MW01194427

STOP BEING INVISIBLE

Overcoming Communication Barriers

Dr. William Lane

Spotlight Publishing

Goodyear, AZ

Stop Being Invisible—Overcoming Communication Barriers
© Copyright William Lane Ed D 2018 First Edition
First Published in the USA by MBK Enterprises, LLC | Spotlight Publishing, Goodyear AZ
ISBN: 978-1-7320727-6-3 Paperback
ISBN: 978-1-7320727-7-0 Ebook
Library of Congress Cataloging-in-Publication Data: Lane, William
Editors:
Becky Norwood, MBK Enterprises, LLC | Spotlight Publishing
Laura Wilkinson

Cover: Angie Anyala
Image: Purchased through Adobe Stock

Interior Layout: Judy Monhollen

Stop Being Invisible! Overcoming Communication Barriers
1. Self-Help 2. Instructional 3. Speaking and Communicating

Dr. William Lane, Ed D
www.drlaneedconsultant.com
www.StopBeingInvisible.com

TABLE OF CONTENTS

Opportunity Section:

> List five "attention-getting statements" that you feel would help assist and benefit you to listen and participate more.
>
> Name the people with whom you will share these statements.

Opportunity Section:

> List five ways you are using technology to avoid human companionship.
>
> What are you missing in life because of it?
>
> List five ways you are using technology to connect with others or stay informed.

Opportunity Section:

> Describe five times you have used technology to escape face-to-face interaction
>
> Discuss how these actions have interfered with a relationship.

Opportunity Section:

> What are three ways you try to focus attention on yourself?
>
> List instances where your need for attention has caused you or others problems.
>
> Describe situations where you have observed other people focusing attention on themselves to the exclusion of others.

Opportunity Section:

> List three instances where your communication was not clear; and how it caused you problems.

> List three instances where the communication with others was not clear; what problems did it cause you as the receiver?

> List three ideas you will use to increase the clarity of your communication, both as the sender and the receiver.

Opportunity Section:

> Describe three times where you have added a comment, to a conversation, that seemed to be a "conversation killer".

> List two "self-statements" you can make to yourself that will cause thinking before you speak.

Opportunity Section:

> As the sender; give three examples where you asked a question and got a one-word response.

> Rephrase each question to receive a more informative answer.

> As the receiver, give three examples where you answered a question using only one word as your answer.

> Using these same examples, how could you have phrased your answers to provide a better response?

Opportunity Section:

> What are the five ways you are opting out of communicating with others?

> What negative impact has opting out caused you?

> What behaviors of yours have caused others to opt out of communicating with you?

> What negative impact did this cause for you?

Opportunity Section:

What missed opportunities have you experienced due to your lack of effective communication skills?

Can you identify the basis for why you missed out? Was it; fear of embarrassment, being told you could not do something, feeling your response would not be "good enough," etc.?

Was the opportunity worth missing? Explain.

What is the "worst that could have happened" had you taken advantage of the missed opportunity?

Give at least two examples of how you would have or could have communicated differently.

Opportunity Section:

What is the main area of the communication process that is the most difficult for you?

What other areas also cause you to stop communicating?

What steps can you take to improve your communication skills?

Opportunity Section:

What actions or phrases will help you become more focused when communicating?

Opportunity Section:

List ways you chose to isolate yourself from communicating with others.

What positive steps can you take to open the communication process as both a sender and receiver?

What benefits do you expect will happen as a result of these changes?

Opportunity Section:

List the actions you will take to make yourself volunteer more.

Opportunity Section:

How have you grown from this communication experience?

List examples to show why more practice is needed or that you are ready to perform this skill on a regular basis.

What area(s) within the communication process do you need to practice?

List the skill(s) you are going to practice.

What strategy will you use to make these skill(s) permanent?

Opportunity Section:

What is the first communication skill you want to improve? Why?

Use the progress chart to establish goals for yourself and to chart your success.

Communication Goals

Opportunity Section:

List any additional communication goals you may want to work on.

Opportunity Section:

Use the questions below to evaluate your communication encounters

For successful communication experiences:

What was something I did that made this communication experience successful?

Using this experience to learn from others

What did I learn (take away) from this communication experience?

How have I grown from this successful communication experience?

For less-than-successful communication experiences:

What was something I may have said or done to make this communication experience less than successful?

Opportunity Section:

List communication situations that make you feel stressed.

Opportunity Section:

> Are you hearing or listening during a conversation? Explain your answer.
>
> List five things you can do to make yourself a better listener.

Opportunity Section:

> List five things you could do that would make you a better communicator.

Opportunity Section:

> List three ways you will become a better listener

> Use this chart when you want to interact with someone.

Opportunity Section:

> List the subjects that you think are your conversational strengths.
>
> List other subjects you would like to add as conversational strengths.

Opportunity Section:

> List five different ways to open/start a conversation with another individual.

Opportunity Section:

> Extend the conversation.

Respond to these statements made by another person to "keep the
conversation going."

Opportunity Section:
What are three topics you might use to be a Table Star?

Opportunity Section:
What are some ways you can make your name tag memorable?
Use the space below to practice designing a name tag.

Opportunity Section:
List five open-ended questions that you might ask someone.

Opportunity Section:
Watch a news program and list five open-ended questions that were asked.

Opportunity Section:
Turning closed questions into open-ended questions

Opportunity Section:
Change these negative questions into positive questions

Opportunity Section:
Bubble chart questions

Opportunity Section:

    List ten compliments you could give to someone.

    List ten compliments you could give to yourself.

Opportunity Section:

    What have you wanted to accomplish but have been held back because you keep overanalyzing the situation?

Opportunity Section:

    Pick two quotes to carry around with you to encourage your success.

ACKNOWLEDGMENTS

This book would have been many pages longer were I to acknowledge **ALL** those who helped in this mighty endeavor.

Kristen—There is little that can be done to repair the past, and the words "I am sorry" do not even come close to my true feelings. Being a better communicator for the past few years does not even come close to equating to the years where I was a non-communicative participant in "your" conversations.

Shelley—Had you not suggested that "I put my knowledge to good use and help others," I am not sure I would have ever become an author.

Adidas—You sat on my lap, or right next to the computer while I toiled away hour after hour, sometimes forgetting to feed either of us. I appreciate you being with me throughout the whole process.

Leonora—Thank you for recognizing my sincere and heartfelt desire to help others with ASD. Also, for inviting me to speak at the ANCA World Festival, and to be a presenter at the ANCA World Tour.

David—After hearing you speak about how important communication skills are, I could not wait to further discuss your experiences. You provided me with the desire to continue writing.

Mrs. P.—Thank you for the opportunity to speak with David. My book is done! It is now time to start on a book about David.

Debi, Pete, and Anne—My sincere thanks to each of you for the endless time spent proofreading, editing, and making suggestions.

Ryan—I appreciated your constant interest about the progress of "The Book".

Courtney—Thank you for the many times you shared your technical knowledge and expertise. On my return from Vancouver, you suggested that "I write a book." Here is that book!

Josh—You shared your technical knowledge and expertise on so many occasions during this process. Thank you!

PURPOSE

The purpose of this book is to provide me with the opportunity to share how having limited communication abilities affected my life and, more importantly, those around me. After speaking with other people, I realized that there were many others whose lives had been affected to some degree by the lack of effective communication skills. You are the inspiration for this book and for my mission to help people learn to communicate and express themselves and improve their quality of life.

Many say that all stories have a "why" and a "how." My "why" occurred one day when, during a conversation, it was brought to my attention that I was nothing more than a "weatherman." How odd, I thought, and I questioned what they meant. While the response I got was not kind, in other ways, it was my wakeup call to change my communication practices. During this conversation, I was told that no one wanted to talk to me, pure and simple, and *also very blunt*.

Most people avoided talking to me because, usually, the only time I contributed to a conversation was when I asked about how their weather was. This person emphatically stated that during their conversations and those others had with me; everyone else was doing ninety-plus percent of the talking. I was just listening and on a rare occasion would participate. It was stated that when I did participate, my question was almost always

"How is the weather there?" After asking this "stock" question, that was the end of my participation, leaving the burden of the "carrying on the conversation" to others. Often, they got annoyed or bored and ended the conversation, leaving me feeling more isolated than before. The ending statement of this conversation was that everyone dreaded even having to *call and talk to me*, so it was not just an in-person problem.

At first, I thought this was just being said in anger. However, after some deep thought, I realized, and those around me would agree, that I could be a very difficult person to communicate with and understand. Whether in the role of dad, husband, boyfriend, brother, uncle, cousin, friend, coach and all the many other roles in life I assumed, few people had been able to understand my non-communicative style.

This powerful and descriptive one-sided revelation of how others felt about having me as part of their conversation made me realize there needed to be a change. I thought that being a good listener and listening to them talk was what I was supposed to do. It was then I realized how I was choosing to participate in conversations; by becoming a "non-participant."

This non-participatory approach may have been a residual effect from when I was a young child. How many of us remember being told "this is an adult conversation," or "talk only when you are spoken to"? Statements like these and others would make me feel conflicted about which conversations I should join and which ones I should merely observe. Whether the comments were said in jest or as a deterrent from having the children speak, for me, as the message receiver, I became self-conscious about speaking and inhibited in my participation in any conversation. These statements, I am sure, were contributors to the reasons I chose not to participate in conversations.

Having low self-esteem and being less assertive because I did not feel comfortable communicating may have also been a contributing factor.

How could I feel comfortable expressing my thoughts when I feared being cut off with those phrases I remembered from childhood? There were other factors in my childhood and adult life that were equally influential in discouraging me from taking an active role in most conversations.

As I grew older, thoughts from my childhood of when and where I should speak still influenced my ability to be a contributing member in any conversation. My "failure to contribute" stemmed from my belief that I had nothing worthwhile or productive to contribute. This "failure," and other's imposed and self-perceived impressions were *not* true, and I was determined to diligently work to improve my ability to communicate. I *did* have something worthwhile to contribute. It was time, and long overdue, for me to become an active participant in conversations and not let everyone else do all the talking. Of course, it was also not my intention to become the center of every conversation to the exclusion of others, merely to participate more.

My use of these statements (and others), "I agree," "That is a really good point," "That is something I had never thought about," helped me become a contributing member to many conversations. I no longer wanted to be called "the weatherman" behind my back or to my face. Instead, my desire was to become someone whom others felt comfortable calling and having a conversation with. I wanted to have people "want" to call me rather than *dread* calling me.

A second "why" occurred recently when I heard a young man named David speak about how much his life had changed when he realized the importance of having good communication skills. David is a Special Olympian athlete whom I had the privilege of meeting at a Special Olympics luncheon. He spoke about how his life had greatly changed when he started working to improve his communication skills. During a one-on-one interview we had, David shared how, as an employee working at a large hardware store, he needs to be able to greet and assist customers.

When asked what he found most helpful, he spoke about the ways his school and his teachers helped him improve his communication skills. Topics of conversation were scripted for him so that he could practice communicating with others. He had the opportunity to practice his social skills in a controlled setting and then would be placed in different social settings to practice what he had learned.

My thanks to David for showing me that there were many others who could benefit from a book on improving communication skills.

FOREWORD

Please allow me to introduce myself. My name is Christopher Lehman, a practitioner of education for children from birth to 21 years. My professional career spans over 23 years, two states, and four school districts. I have an earned BS in Kinesiological Studies, a MA in Early Childhood Education, and a Graduate Certificate in School Administration.

Six years ago, Dr. Bill Lane pulled me out of the shadows of educational practice in the field of special education as a teacher and administrator and into the world of higher education. It was here in this world where I too, along with his leadership, have helped guide and shape the practice and professionalism of future educational practitioners.

One class in particular was instrumental during our initial collaboration, named: Functional Communication for Students with Autism and Severe Disabilities. It was through this content on brain development, encompassing the powerful reflection on the role communication has in all of our lives, and when impairment due to disability or stressors/factors that render ineffectiveness of our communication systems where much of my own reflection revealed itself. I am forever grateful for the opportunities that have ensued over the past six years, all because Dr. Bill Lane, or Bill as we have become friends as well as professional colleagues, afforded me the platform.

By creating *Stop Being Invisible!*, Bill has now extended this opportunity to all of you. The book guides you through opportunities to work on your lines of communication in areas where you find there are needs, gaps, or necessary improvements. Bill has written a thought-provoking, self-reflecting, and interactive book providing you the opportunities to improve your modes of communication.

Personally, for me, this plays true when entering into a situation with people where, a) I do not have a common interaction with and/or b) Are associated with professions not directly in line with education.

Chapter 3, <u>WAY TOO GOOD AT NOT TALKING</u>, provides insight into Bill's practice of becoming way too good at not talking! Here, he reflects on a summation of interactions and specifically writes this: *"By letting someone else do the talking, I didn't have to worry that what I would say was incorrect or that my input would not be valued. I was happy living in this no commitment state of being, where no disapproval could come my way by not speaking. As I would later experience, nothing was further from the truth!"*

My struggle was the opportunities I was in were with individuals engaged with the business and financial fields. These were very different from my educational background. I made a choice to learn more about both of those realms and attempted to draw a connection between that and education. It was soon that I realized that I was doing all of the work in preparation for these encounters; for which I later realized, were actually opportunities.

In Chapter 4, <u>COULD I OPT OUT?</u>, specifically, when reading the following two sentences, I immediately reflected on where I too had originated from within my history of communication: *"Isolating myself from others was no longer the way I wanted to live my life."* And *"By improving my communication skills, I was hoping to possibly have a chance to restructure my life into one worth living. I realized that way too many missed opportunities had occurred and it was now time for me to <u>Stop Being Invisible!</u>"*

As I continued reading Chapter 4, (as is with all of his chapters) I actually used the **OPPORTUNITY SECTION**, which included the following questions: What are five ways you are opting out of communicating with others? What negative impact has opting out caused you? What behaviors of yours have caused others to opt out of communicating with **_you_**? What negative impact did this cause for you? Then, reading ahead, the last section describes the missed opportunities that occurred through opting out of communication opportunities and choosing to be invisible. This was a great summation of my personal reflection as I read Chapter 4.

Bill has written _Stop Being Invisible!_ in a manner that you sense you are sitting with him at a coffee table exchanging and sharing stories with each other. The personal reflections he provides truly opens the doors for you to reflect on your own and connect with someone else who has lived through the self-identification and self-reflection to now being the viable person of pro-active interactive communication. Earlier I wrote, how I decided to conduct research into the professions of those I was interacting with on a more consistent basis.

Bill reinforced this strategy for me in Chapter 9: TAKE YOUR TIME—START SMALL, where he described a technique where he chose to listen to others in conversation and then, make a chart of the people and their interests. Empowered with his knowledge of people and content, Bill was able to step-in and join the conversation with similar knowledge, this too was a strategy I used, and Bill affirmed it.

As you, continue reading _Stop Being Invisible!_ you are encouraged and afforded the opportunity to apply your reflections and readings into each chapter as they build on each other until the end. Through Bill's interpersonal expressions, you are drawn into real world examples of the barriers and disabilities that have affected a real person in his real world in his words! Bill's use of positive voice and connectivity through all of the chapters draws you into a sense of reflection and desire to answer the questions throughout all of the opportunity sections in each chapter. The beauty of the book is the accessibility to return to individual chapters when needed for further reflection to constantly improve. Once you see the impact of your work through Bill's words, you too will be happy to engage with others the experiences you have allowed yourself to engage.

It is my hope that my messages that I have shared here with you will help in fueling the excitement of reading *Stop Being Invisible!* Yet, more importantly, it is my hope that I have inspired you to ENGAGE with the book!!

Let me leave you with two of Bill's final quotes from Chapter 16 in his book and one of my favorites:

Chapter 16:

"Communication is a skill that you can learn. It's like riding a bicycle or typing. If you're willing to work at it, you can rapidly improve the quality of every part of your life."

—Brian Tracy

"If you just communicate, you can get by. But if you communicate skillfully, you can work miracles."

—Jim Rohn

One of my favorites I tend to share when teaching and presenting:

"It's the repetition of affirmations that leads to belief. And once that belief becomes a deep conviction things begin to happen."

—Muhammad Ali

Here is to your future affirmations and beliefs as things will begin to happen in your lives!

Thank you for time and attention.

Christopher Lehman,

Education Associate, Delaware Department of Education

PREFACE

"The quality of your life is the quality of your communication."

—Tony Robbins

Stop Being Invisible is for anyone who feels the desire to improve their face-to-face communicative interaction in this "age of technology." With communication guiding a large part of everyone's life, the ability to increase one's communication skills is becoming a contributing factor to one's success in life. In other words, without the development of the necessary communication skills, there can be a low probability of success or the enjoyment of life.

Stop Being Invisible is a personal reflection on experiences and the impact having limited communication skills has had on my life. Segments of this book are from fifty-plus years of a life where I was seldom understood by those with whom I tried to associate or communicate. This was through no fault of theirs but because of my unwillingness to attempt to share my thoughts and feelings with anyone. Others thought that I did not want to speak to them or that I did not love them enough to find a way to communicate. In fact, the reason was quite the opposite. I did not know how!

As you read, **Stop Being Invisible**, you will be able to visualize and comprehend how my inability to communicate not only impacted me but those around me. You will gain insight, and learn about the trials and tribulations throughout my life because of my communication difficulties.

Most sections are filled with at least one example based on my own life experiences, thus allowing the reader to visualize the point being shared. A large part of the examples are from direct memory, while a few have been re-created from memory or shared because of the hurt they either caused to others or me personally.

For confidentiality purposes, I have changed some of the names of others whom I refer to in the book.

At the end of some sections, I have shared with the reader example(s) of a specific communication difficulty followed by ways to recognize, minimize, and apply the suggestions I have used. My knowledge and experiences of the strategies, techniques, and ideas these communication problems caused will also be discussed. Throughout the book, "opportunity exercises" are provided that encourage the reader to practice improving a particular aspect of their communication skills. You are highly encouraged to take advantage of these exercises.

My struggle with poor communication skills is self-admitted. On numerous occasions, and sometimes it was venomously expressed, I was the subject of those who felt my desire to isolate myself was voluntary. Your knowledge and understanding of the hurtfulness this has caused in my life is important, and it is probably something you have experienced first-hand. With this understanding, your awareness and application of some of the ideas, suggestions, and techniques discussed will hopefully provide you with methods to reach beyond the darkness and alienation your communication struggles are causing you.

This book has taken a lifetime to write, and my wish is that my experiences, which I internalized and then projected onto others, will be a guide for improving your own communication skills. If **Stop Being Invisible** can ignite just one tidbit or "knowledge nugget" that helps you experience some amount of improvement in your communication skills, then I will have achieved my purpose for writing this book.

If you would like to learn what I have done to change my personal communication skills, how I have progressed to feel more comfortable in social situations, how my relationships have improved, and how I discovered a greater sense of confidence and more self-esteem, and want to use these to improve your communication skills, then this book is for **YOU!**

INTRODUCTION

When Dr. Bill Lane began writing this book, his intended audience was individuals who have been diagnosed or are self-diagnosed as having Autism Spectrum Disorder (ASD) tendencies. He realized the importance of assisting them to improve their communication and social skills to become more fully engaged and contributing members to their family, friends, and society. As the work progressed, he realized the beneficial aspects to a wider range of individuals, namely anyone desiring to improve their communication skills.

Bill has chosen to share his life's story as testimony that having communication difficulties can impact many parts of a person's life. Unless someone is willing to take the steps necessary to change, his or her life will be a continuing disconnection from family, friends, and society. In Stop Being Invisible, Bill has assembled a collection of examples, ideas, skills, and techniques that he has successfully implemented to improve his communication difficulties. By sharing his first-hand perspective, he hopes that others can use this information to strengthen their own communication skills.

The writing is direct and informative, as the author shares numerous examples throughout the book to illustrate important concepts based on his personal experiences. As a former educator and now an Educational Consultant, Bill has written this book so that individuals understand there are a variety of ideas, methods, strategies, and techniques one can use to overcome their communication obstacles. Based on his personal experiences, these tactics have proven to be effective in helping him meet his goals for improving his communication difficulties, thus leading to more social interactions and further satisfactory involvement in society.

CHAPTER 1:

WHAT IS COMMUNICATION?

*"Communication—the human connection—is the key to
personal and career success."*

—Paul J. Meyer

Communication is the transferring of information from the speaker (message sender) to the listener (message receiver). The word "communication" is derived from the Latin word "communis," meaning to share. (A special thank you, Mrs. Levitt! Students who were fortunate enough to have Mrs. Levitt as an English teacher, know exactly what I mean.) Communication is a two-way process that involves at least one sender in a manner that allows for message delivery that is clear and successful, and by at least one listener who receives and understands.

Of the two parts of the communication process (sending and receiving), the sending of the message was never the difficult part for me because I rarely cared to send any messages. Instead, I expected others to send the message to which I would choose to respond or ignore. A vast majority, in fact, ALL of the messages that were sent, I chose to ignore. The receiving and understanding of the message being sent was the difficult part of the process for me. Whether I was choosing not to want to receive the message ("Why do I care about what you are saying/What is its significance to me?", or sarcastically thinking "That is REALLY nice"...or being able to understand the message being sent ("What are you talking about?") all were contributing factors to mine and others opinions that I possessed a "failure to communicate".

This failure to respond appropriately was probably rooted in my low self-esteem (as previously referenced). My thought process was, why would anybody be interested in anything I *would have to say?* Or, thinking that the answers provided by others would be better than mine so why should I bother them with my response? It's just a thought on my part as to a reason you may have chosen to ignore communications.

As I reflect back on this past problem, it seems like the reason for the failure of this successful transferring of information occurred because one or more of the participants was not stating the purpose of their communication to me. In other words, "why was this communication occurring"?

For me, had the speaker explained the purpose of the communication, or at least alluded to its purpose, this may have provided me a reason to listen. In the same way, a memo includes a subject or RE: line that identifies the topic or intention of the memo. Had the message sender started the conversation with statements similar to those stated in the example below, they would have been providing me with a purpose of tuning into or participating in the conversation.

For me, the use of these "attention-getting statements," introducing the topic, if you will, would have brought new meaning, an alert so to speak, for my needing to more carefully focus my attention to the message being sent. Instead, my feeling of having no rationale to care about a conversation supported my thoughts that I could just opt out of any and all communications.

On many occasions, I was too distracted by the myriad of other activities going on to focus on what one particular person was saying. These distractions included the conversation of other people nearby, the music on the radio, etc. When I finally did realize that I was being included in a conversation that was occurring and that I should be tuned into, I had no clue what was being discussed and, therefore, had no interest and could not see how the conversation required my participation. Entering into the middle of conversations about which I had no idea of the topic was something I chose not to do.

Making "attention-getting statements" to gain their students' attention is a common practice for many educators. Here are just a few samples of the many that can be used: "One, two, three, eyes on me" "Hocus Pocus-Everyone Focus," "Who is ready to rock and roll?"

For me, I found it most beneficial when people would start their conversation with statements similar to these:

- "I want to share this (funny, interesting, serious, etc.) story with you"
- "What I am going to tell you is important!"
- "It is necessary that you understand what we are going to be talking about because...."
- "You need to listen carefully to this next..."
- "Here is why you need to listen to what I am saying..."
- "I want to know what your thoughts are..."

OR, if someone noticed that I was not paying attention to a conversation and made an attempt to draw my attention back to the topic of the conversation and also provide a quick recap of the conversation like; "Bill, our conversation is about Japan and we were wondering if you would share some of your experiences since you were over there for four years." Statements like these would have made it easier for me to see the rationale for my participation, help me participate in a "partially missed" conversation, or resume an active listening role in the communication process.

OPPORTUNITY SECTION:

List five "attention-getting statements" that you feel would help assist and benefit you to listen and participate more.

_____

_____

_____

_____

_____

_____

Name the people with whom you will share these statements.

_____

_____

_____

_____

_____

_____

ARE WE LOSING OUR NEED FOR COMPANIONSHIP?

Effective communication is becoming a "lost art." New technology and social media are having a negative impact on our social activities, including our personal and professional relationships. Mental health issues associated with the overuse of this new technology and social media have been widely reported and include, among other examples:

- cyber-bullying
- suicidal thoughts
- sleep deprivation
- exposure to unsuitable material

As the world continues to grow more connected electronically and the forms and means by which people can "communicate" continue to expand, good communication skills are essential for success. It is necessary for us to change how we handle our daily communication with those with whom we interact. Good communication skills are needed for success in our lives, relationships with family and friends, and while interacting with others at work.

Many employers require that their employees possess strong communication skills. The need for effective communication skills has become the number one most desired "soft skill" by employers. Face-to-face communication is becoming less and less of a necessity as the time available to communicate is shrinking. We need to learn to use this limited time together more effectively. The use of words to transfer specific meanings sets humans apart from the rest of the animal kingdom. Of all the life skills we possess, the ability to communicate is the most important. For human interaction to occur, there must be some form of communication.

It becomes more apparent on a daily basis that we live in a technical society where many people choose to communicate electronically. No matter where you look, many people have a technological device in their hand or very close to them and appear to be hooked on their "smart phones." When you look at couples, families, and groups of teenagers, most of them are focused on their electronic devices rather than communicating face-to-face. Even young children can be seen operating tablets and other electronic devices.

Technology should not always be viewed as a negative, Apple's CEO, Tim Cook during a CNN exclusive interview stated his feelings for the use of technology as wanting people to be satisfied and empowered by their devices. My five-year-old grandson Logen has begun to realize the exciting possibilities that technology can have on learning. His favorite gift at Christmas was an iPad™ that contained information about dinosaurs, thus allowing him to delve deeply into one of his favorite subjects.

My three-year-old granddaughter, Colbie can maneuver her way to find any of her many desired apps on an iPad™ better than I can. She will often look at me with a puzzled look when she cannot find the app, asks me for help, and I cannot figure out what to do. Older people (and we know who we are) know that any questions we have about technology can be answered by a teenager more quickly and easily than finding the answers by ourselves.

Are people addicted to the little glowing screen of their electronic devices? Much has been written about the effects of using these devices. There is discussion about people becoming "addicted," having the feeling of disconnectedness, and possibly even personality changes from the effects of using our electronic devices. I have heard people who have described their friends as "hooked on high tech" and "social media addicts." Could the use of technology possibly be interfering with our ability to interact socially with others? Have we become a society

where people purposefully "connect but at the same time also isolate" themselves from others?

Some people think so, and because of this belief and the potential for harm, apps are now being developed to allow those "hooked" on their electronic devices to break their "addiction occasionally." An article I recently read suggested that smartphones are the new cigarettes, with the writer comparing these newly developed apps to a new kind of nicotine patch. Some argue that it is the media and technology companies' obligation to acknowledge the harm potential of their products and help by working to mitigate it. Recently, iPhone's™ maker, Apple™ released a statement saying, "We think deeply about how our products are used and the impact they have on users and the people around them."

Others feel that people have no addiction to their phones or electronic devices. They feel that the devices serve to cognitively remind us of our connectedness, provide us our identity, and provide both a sense of security and control. They believe that the most important and underappreciated value of the phone is its ability to connect us to one another. These people argue that there is a need to understand the effect of taking away the devices, and what it would mean to individuals and society. If people could not use technology to connect, stay informed, and entertain themselves, there may be some loss of psychological benefits. These psychological benefits that technology provides for humans' well-being are having social connections and the core human needs for information and entertainment. They believe the important point to consider is what the phone is being used for, not the worry of addiction.

Rarely do we find people sitting and talking to each other; instead, we see each person's focus is on their electronic device. When was the last time you ate a meal with others without a phone present?

How many times do you see entire families sitting at a table at a restaurant and rather than having a conversation with each other, they are all on their devices? Disconnecting from our phones allows us the opportunity to reconnect with the people and things we most value. "A phone is everyone's vaccination against an awkward conversation. It does not have to ping. It is just there to grab at any moment", said Marlene Sokol. * Tampa Bay Times 10/24/2017

"By 2020, the average person will have more conversations with their "bots" than with their spouse."

SOURCE: GARTNER'S TOP 10 STRATEGIC PREDICTIONS FOR 2017 AND BEYOND—GARTNERS SYMPOSIUM/ITXPO 2016

Example: While eating dinner one night with a friend, her cell phone "beeped." She immediately excused herself from the table to "check her message." Less than a minute later, she again excused herself to check on the status of her computer which was being repaired remotely. Her cell phone beeped again, and she moved to see what that message was. These and various other technological interruptions continued for about the next ten minutes. Due to her constantly being distracted by her electronic devices, I was able to finish my dinner and went into the other room. You can imagine her surprise when she looked across the table, and I was not there. She had not even noticed my leaving.

OPPORTUNITY SECTION:

List five ways you are using technology to avoid human companionship.

_____

_____

_____

_____

_____

What are you missing in your life because of it?

_____

_____

_____

_____

_____

List five ways you are using technology to connect with others or stay informed.

_____

_____

_____

_____

_____

ONE DAY WITHOUT A CELL PHONE

One day without a cell phone is something that Tiffany Southwell, an English teacher at Steinbrenner High School, has suggested to students in her classes for the past six years. It is a strictly voluntary assignment where her students would give her their cell phones for a day and afterward write her an essay about their feelings and experiences during their "disconnected phase." Students in the class were reading Ray Bradbury's 1953 novel, Fahrenheit 451. The objective of this assignment: would Bradbury's futuristic world, where books were burned, be relatable in 2017? Would one day without their cell phone cause the students to end up like Clarisse or Montag, questioning the values of society and appreciate the simple things of life?

Here are some of the responses taken from the students' essays submitted to Ms. Southwell. They were reported in a newspaper article from The Tampa Bay Times dated October Twenty-fourth, 2017. Chase Jackson wrote, "People are going too fast and don't take time to observe things and enjoy the luxuries of life." "When people are always on their phone, they are not observing anything else." John Kahyaoglu wrote, "I literally thought that it was the end of the world." Another student, Jennifer Vazquez, wrote that she started having symptoms of physical withdrawal: jumpiness, irritability, then a headache. She described it as being "like having a weight over your head."

For those students who chose to participate in Ms. Southwell's assignment, lunch was an exercise in endurance. Jackson noted "nearly half of Steinbrenner High School is generally in one area, and people are still not talking to each other physically. Instead, they are 'stuffing their faces' and scrolling through their phones." Kai'Rell Lewis, in describing his bus ride home, wrote, "It was the longest bus ride of my life." Another student, McKenna Leist, wrote, "I felt disconnected in a weird sense, almost like I was part of 'some other world' that required my attention, but I was cut off from." MJ Aljuboori was upset because he could not watch his cat videos.

Not all of the responses described negative experiences. Others participating in the assignment, such as Bobby Harrigan, had the opportunity to talk with his parents and his sister. Sebastian Maceda, who thought his attachment to the phone was just "a teenage thing," noticed that this same attachment was true for his father, mother, sister, and brother. Football player, Harrison Klein, learned that after practice he could speak with a teammate about something other than football. "We talked about school and what he does when he is not playing or watching football." Other students reported they had slept better, and Lauren Donahey wrote, "I felt this feeling of serenity, comfort, and contentment." One even told the teacher, "if I did not have a phone, I would be a rock star in school."

Ms. Southwell stated that "The reflective discussion basically has been the same for the past six years. The students admit they have unhealthy obsessions with their phones. They notice how anxious they become when they can't check it, and how many times they check it for no reason at all. Students noticed that they ignore their families, blow off homework assignments, constantly check their phones while driving, and miss out on actual communication with others." "My students acknowledge they have a problem. They also admit they do not have the willpower to do anything about this problem..."

OPPORTUNITY SECTION:

Describe five times you have used technology to escape face-to-face interaction.

_____

_____

_____

_____

_____

_____

Discuss how these actions have interfered with a relationship.

_____

_____

_____

_____

_____

The bottomline is that there is a need for balance when it comes to technology. Technology is not bad in and of itself. When people use technology as a means to avoid conversation or interaction it becomes an issue, much like an addiction.

CHAPTER 2:

PEOPLE'S DESIRE FOR ATTENTION

In sharp contrast to the non-attention seeking, isolated world that I previously desired to exist in, there are people today who have an insatiable lust for attention. Often, it appears that they are only happy when they are getting attention from others. Even though a person's desire for attention may be "satisfied" by these actions or others, let us consider that others can easily follow our actions.

With the rapid advances in technology and the limited amount of time between when an event occurs to when it appears on media platforms, people can easily and quickly get recognition. These actions, knowingly or unknowingly taken, can bring them this attention. Is it worth the results? Unfortunately, they do not recognize the difference between being *positively* recognized and negative recognition. For them, the desire is just to get ATTENTION!

Example: There are people who appear in various forms of media with the desire for people to like them. They will agree with an article that might gain them this person's admiration, but it may cause harm and hurt feelings to others who do not support this statement, or they might even be examples that disprove the lumping of all based on the actions of a few (stereotyping). They will quickly agree with some point of view or statement they might not necessarily support but will agree and respond to be accepted.

Example: Some people in their need for attention will feel that by copying the latest "headline" newsmaker, they too will get recognized. They only observe how much media coverage is dedicated to this action. They think that making a statement will attract the attention they are seeking. They don't stop to consider the consequences that have occurred or will occur to "yesterday's news sensation."

Example: Another interesting desire some people have is to brag about having many "friends, followers, or connections" they have on the different sites. People will brag about having ten thousand connections, thousands of followers, or even hundreds of friends. Whether the "connections" are of value does not enter their mind. They do not think about "quality," only "quantity."

OPPORTUNITY SECTION:

What are three ways that you try to focus attention on yourself?

_____

_____

_____

_____

_____

_____

List instances where your need for attention has caused you or others problems.

_____

_____

_____

_____

_____

_____

Describe situations where you have observed other people focusing the attention on themselves to the exclusion of others.

_____

_____

_____

_____

_____

BE CAREFUL WHAT YOU SAY, SHARE, POST, BLOG, TWEET, etc.!

In today's social media age, there appears to not only be the need for attention but also the need for instant connection with others. Many people are constantly "on" their social media accounts, writing more, but communicating less and less. These people take pride in the number of "friends" they have, or the latest events happening in someone else's life.

When they receive a notice about a new friend or connection, they cannot wait to respond. Their haste to respond sometimes causes misunderstandings and misspellings. This need to respond quickly can often occur during inopportune circumstances (i.e., driving, during meetings, when others may not want a response, etc.) and may result in serious consequences.

Everyone has the right to free speech, but there are consequences. Responding before thinking about how you want to respond and what you want to say may influence how the receiver will interpret your message and can have serious consequences.

Being on social media should not be a reason for saying whatever you want about others. One general rule I have learned about communication, sometimes the hard way, is to be careful about expressing the first thought that comes to your mind (this includes communicating via technology). This immediate response problem has been described as OTM...OTM. "On the mind...Out the mouth."

Although our first thoughts are usually our true feelings, at that moment, once they are out, they are out! What may happen is that they regret what they shared. Taking a tweet, post, blog, etc. down after you realize how people have responded is like publishing it on the front page of a newspaper. You can be held for libel or slander.

Here are some examples of how they may try to retract communications:

- apologizing
- trying to delete the post
- expressing regret
- saying that the message was "misunderstood"
- saying that was not "their voice"
- claiming they were not the one who posted the communication
- claiming they were on drugs

No matter which of these they use, there is no taking it back. Once it is said, it is out there! It can and will have been seen, heard, and remembered by someone. Not only that, it might be accessible years later, and there is the possibility that it could and might be used against you. Even if you delete something…you still said it and still wrote it!

I have learned that, as the message sender, I must be careful and think about the message being sent and the impact the message will have on the receiver. I have learned that I am not alone in this problem, I have plenty of company. We have all, from time to time, written or said something that caused a problem. We are, after all, human.

The key issue is "occasional" versus "chronic"; if you are always sending apologies or chasing after your words, you may have a chronic problem. One way to lessen this problem is to focus on the meaning of what you want to communicate to the person receiving the message. As the sender, it is your responsibility to increase the chances of your message being understood.

Considering how the message could be interpreted by other people has helped me become a sender of clearer and more complete messages. Using the process of clear and thoughtful communication can help you avoid possible misunderstanding or conflict about the sent message. Before sending the message, ask yourself:

1.　　"Will the other person perceive the message as I intended?" and

2.   "Have I clearly stated my meaning?"

As the sender, you should be able to answer both of these questions positively. While these questions might not solve all misunderstandings, you are proactively taking steps to avoid misinterpretations.

Here are some practical examples on the issue of intent.

Example: While working as a school administrator I would often hear students say to each other, "You are fat!" "Your ears are not the same size," "You smell."

Although these statements may have been said in anger or were, in the mind of the message sender, true statements, consider the impact these messages had on the receiver. Think about the hurt the receiver felt; would they still want to associate with you or be your friend? How would you feel about being on the receiving end of what you're about to say?

Example: One of the problems that can occur when communicating electronically is that the receiver is expected to understand the text, post, in whatever form the information is being conveyed, in the way it was intended. This is not always the case. Sometimes a text will be sent where the words used are very negative, yet a smiley face or some other emoji is placed at the end of the message, and the receiver is now unsure of the message's intent.

Remember: Once something is said or written, you can wish it had not been, you can apologize for your actions and regret your actions, but you can never take it back! Immediate responses tend to lead to a lack of intelligent debate on a subject or idea, but may also be seen as an attack on the sender.

Federal, state, and local police agencies are taking this matter very seriously. States have laws in effect to deal with this issue. Here is a portion of a press release from the Delaware State Police as an example of their seriousness for these actions:

All online or verbal threats toward a school will result in serious consequences. It is important to know the Delaware State Police will dedicate resources to investigate each one regardless of the person's intent. The responsibility for keeping our schools safe belongs to everyone in the community. Parents, Schools and Law Enforcement play a key role to ensure schools are safe learning environments.

Parents who remain vigilant with their children's online activities and social media sites may detect unusual behaviors and prevent potential problems. Parents can help by implementing certain parameters like rules and expectations of their children and watching for any warning signs that your teen may be in trouble. Keeping the lines of communication open, staying involved and connected are some of the best ways to prevent bad teen behavior.

Schools continue to help by enhancing student-teacher relationships in hopes of noticing unusual behavior and building trust, so students are more apt to share information. While our school's districts have measures in place to deal with and prevent threats and other emergency situations, it is on all of us to do our part. We have to deal with threats in the appropriate manner so children can learn in a safe environment. Currently, more teenagers face severe charges for online and verbal threats against schools, students, and staff.

Usually, students who make these threats will be identified and interviewed by the police. A comprehensive investigation will be conducted for each violation of the law whether the intent was a hoax or more importantly a real threat. School Resource Officers and Detectives will respond to all online and verbal threats and will conduct a lawful search of the suspect's person, locker, vehicle and residence for items that could be used in an actual attack like weapons, firearms, written plans or anything suspicious or incriminating. If necessary the FBI will be contacted to assist with the investigation. Even if it's a hoax or a real threat against a school, it is vital to know serious consequences can result, as these threats can cause public panic: •Those responsible can be charged with Terroristic Threatening, Disorderly Conduct, and Cyber Threatening and can be either a class F or G felony which can result in prison time and/or probation •Severe penalties and fines of $1000 to $2500.

It is imperative to know that any person can be guilty of terroristic threatening if it is likely to cause an evacuation of a school, building, place of assembly, or facility of public transportation. If it causes a serious inconvenience or includes the reckless disregard of the risk of causing terror or serious inconvenience at a daycare facility, nursery or preschool, kindergarten, elementary, secondary or vocational-technical school it can result in a felony arrest.

The crime of Terroristic Threatening can also bring criminal intimidation charges. The fear brought by threatening posts can cause many students and staff to stay home rather than potentially taking the risk of going to school. Many students do not understand the consequences of their actions until they are arrested, charged and put into the juvenile justice system. The consequences would help the student to understand the severity of making threats. Finally, this conviction will follow them and will have to be reported on any job or college application. If students are convicted of a felony and develop a criminal record it could prevent them from joining the military, being accepted into college or it may even interfere with getting a job.

PRESENTED BY THE DIRECTOR OF PUBLIC INFORMATION, SERGEANT RICHARD D. BRATZ RELEASED: 032918 1251

OPPORTUNITY SECTION:

List three examples where you were not clear in your communications and how it caused you problems.

_____

_____

_____

_____

_____

List three instances where the communication of others was not clear; what problems did it cause for you as the receiver?

_____

_____

_____

_____

_____

_____

List three ideas you will use to increase the clarity of your communications, both as the sender and the receiver.

_____

_____

_____

_____

_____

_____

THINK BEFORE YOU SAY IT!

One of the many unfavorable qualities that I needed to change when communicating with other was my inability to refrain from saying that "first thought" that come to mind. Too often when asked a question or while listening to someone else or others conversation, I would have this thought that would be in my mind and I could not hold back. These thoughts would occur for no particular reason, but seemed like something I needed to add to the conversation. When I allowed these thoughts to become part of the conversation, I noticed that were "conversation killers", because the conversation would come to a sudden end and I would be standing there alone.

While it took me a long time to realize what was occurring, I noticed that when I would first stop and think about the comment and not voice the comment out loud, the conversation would continue. I began practicing a thought process that I called "good conversation addition or bad conversation addition". This momentary thought process allowed me to think "was this statement or comment something that would contribute to the conversation or could if possible be offensive or hinder the progress of the conversation".

While this technique of thinking about and withholding your comment until deciding its impact on the conversation is extremely difficulty, I found it very beneficial as it allowed for many of the conversations to progress to a natural conclusion.

Example: While I was writing this section, my phone rang. My first thought was that I should tell the caller that I was busy and hang up. Had this been my response, this person would probably not have ever called me back. Instead, I stopped working and spent the next fifteen minutes talking with them about their day.

OPPORTUNITY SECTION:

Describe three times where you have added a comment, to a conversation, that seemed to be a "conversation killer".

_____

_____

_____

_____

_____

_____

List two "self-statements" you can make to yourself that will cause thinking before you speak.

_____

_____

_____

_____

_____

_____

OPPORTUNITY SECTION:

Describe three times where you have added a comment, to a conversation, that seemed to be a "conversation killer".

_____

_____

_____

_____

_____

List two "self-statements" you can make to yourself that will cause thinking before you speak.

_____

_____

_____

_____

_____

CHAPTER 3:

WAY TOO GOOD AT NOT TALKING

Are you an expert at staying silent during a conversation? I was. Through a combination of the following factors—choosing not to take an active role in the communication process, not having to initiate or participate in a conversation, and being allowed to continue this non-communicative behavior—I became *way too good* at not talking. My thoughts were that if I continued these behaviors, then I would be happy. By letting someone else do the talking, I did not have to worry that what I would say was incorrect or that my input would not be valued. I was happy living in this no commitment state of being, where no disapproval could come my way by not speaking. As I would later experience, nothing was further from the truth!

What I now wish was that someone had shared some ideas, methods, suggestions, and techniques for correction of this hurtful and harmful habit. Everyone just continued to accept, blame or just think that the problem would correct itself over time. Instead, what had happened was I had mastered the art of opting out of conversations, and with that, I was also opting out of much of life.

As an educational consultant, I have discovered that this non-participation in the communication process is becoming an epidemic within society. Parents contact me on a regular basis about their child or children who are choosing to withdraw from the communication process and isolate themselves from others. Since this seems to be a recurring issue, here are three ideas I share with parents to encourage their child or children to more actively participate in the communication process:

- no longer allow them to provide a "Yes" or "No" answer to any question;
- require that their responses to questions are in complete sentences, **and**
- have them start their response by using part of the question.

I have discussed with them how this can be accomplished by asking who, what, where, when, and why questions. These are known as open-ended questions, and they require more than a one-word answer.

Ineffective:

Mom: "How was your day?"
Child's response: "Fine."

Effective:

Mom: "What was the most interesting thing that happened at school today?"
Child's response: "We learned about when dinosaurs lived millions of years ago."

Ineffective:

Mom: "Did you eat lunch?"
Child's response: "Yes."

Effective:

Mom: "What did you have for lunch?"
Child's response "For lunch, I had pizza, carrot sticks, and juice."

In these examples, the sender is asking their question in a way that opens the door to more interaction with the receiver. Sometimes it will take some practice if you still get a one-word answer, but it may be an occasion where the sender has to make a little more effort to draw the receiver into the discussion.

For younger children, you may require them to give an answer that contains a certain number (three, four, etc.) of words.

This style of communication becomes very important with adolescents who naturally start decreasing the amount of information they share with parents and adults. You may still get short answers, but as the sender, you will need to phrase your question in such a way that the receiver cannot escape with a one-word answer. It takes practice, but it will be worth the effort.

OPPORTUNITY SECTION:

As the sender:

Give three examples of where you asked a question and received a one-word response.

_____

_____

_____

_____

_____

_____

Rephrase each question to receive a more informative answer.

_____

_____

_____

_____

_____

_____

As the Receiver:

Give three examples of where you answered questions using only one word as your answer.

_____

_____

_____

_____

_____

_____

_____

Using those same examples, how could you have phrased your answers to provide a better response?

_____

_____

_____

_____

_____

_____

CHAPTER 4:

COULD I OPT OUT?

Unfortunately, I would eventually discover that no matter how hard I tried to insulate myself, there was no "opting out" of communication with others. Despite my best efforts of ignoring, openly rejecting other peoples' attempts to include me in their conversations, or blatantly choosing to isolate myself from others, all these actions did was make me a "socially isolated person."

Through these repeated and numerous attempts at "ignoring others," people still did not understand the message(s) I was communicating. The message I was attempting to send was "leave me alone," "I am bored," "I choose not to communicate with you," etc. The considerably large number of attempts at "opting out" only further proved to me the importance and necessity of communication because everyone still tried to communicate with me.

Despite being called "hard-headed" and "a loner" on more than one occasion, I have since learned that communicating is something that humans do on a daily basis and it makes up a major part of our active and social lives. Choosing not to participate only confirmed the "label(s)" that others had placed on me and that I had placed on myself. I realized that it was now time for me to make a conscious effort to change.

Somewhere, I remember hearing the saying, "the most important relationship you will ever have is with yourself." This powerful statement made me stop and think that since my current approach to communication was not working, maybe I, and not others, needed to change. The change I decided to make was to change and improve my communication skills. Not to satisfy or impress anyone else (they were not my major concern), but for my well-being and attempt to reconnect with those whom I had hurt terribly.

For some, it was too late to apologize for my behaviors, but for others, I saw this as my opportunity to try to make amends.

Isolating myself from others was no longer the way I wanted to live my life. Instead, I chose to attempt to repair what relationships I could and explain why I had acted the way I did. All the while I was doing this, I knew that nothing I did could ever fully help them understand and/or reduce the pain I had inflicted. By improving my communication skills, I was hoping to possibly have a chance to restructure my life into one worth living. I realized that way too many missed opportunities had occurred and it was now time for me to **Stop Being Invisible!**

OPPORTUNITY SECTION:

What are five ways you are opting out of communicating with others?

_____

_____

_____

_____

_____

_____

What negative impact has opting out caused you?

_____

_____

_____

_____

_____

What behaviors of yours have caused others to opt out of communicating with _you_?

_____

_____

_____

_____

_____

_____

What negative impact did this cause for you?

_____

_____

_____

_____

_____

_____

MISSED OPPORTUNITIES

There are times throughout our lives when we may miss the chance to do something because of fear—self-imposed or imposed by others. One of the reasons these missed opportunities may occur is because of a lack of effective communication skills.

During the course of writing this book, I reflected on some of my missed opportunities. Had I known about or just practiced some of the skills within this book, I am sure my life would have been happier and my relationships more fulfilling. Here is a list of some of my missed opportunities. I am sure there are numerous others, but here are a few examples:

Talking to Mickey Mantle (a former baseball player for the New York Yankees and my childhood idol), in Baltimore when he was signing autographs. Because I felt that I did not know what to say or how to approach him, I failed to get his autograph, shake his hand, or get a photograph of us together. Why? Because of my fear of starting a conversation with someone as important as him!

I was in Atlantic City, New Jersey, and was walking past one of the casinos, and Rodney Dangerfield (a well-known comedian) was stepping out of his limousine. Again, not knowing how to start a conversation, I missed the opportunity to shake his hand and get his autograph.

At President-elect Jimmy Carter's Presidential Inauguration, my daughter and I rode in the same elevator with Dennis McCloud, the movie actor. Although he smiled and said hello, I was afraid of saying the wrong thing and totally ignored him. In this case, not only did I miss an opportunity, but the thought of how uncomfortable he must have felt being in an elevator with people who would not even talk to him continues to this day.

When boarding an airplane that has an open seat policy, I used to never want to sit next to someone. I would go as far back in the plane as necessary to find an open row of seats. Since most planes are usually fully booked, someone will eventually ask if the seat next to me was open and I would reply with a "Yes." Avoiding eye contact and conversation was my "modus operandi," my method of operation (MO). Now, when flying alone, I will find any open seat, and at least attempt to start a conversation with the people sitting in the row with me.

Sometimes we are our own worst enemies, but sometimes the influence comes from others. Their past experiences can not only cause them problems, but they can also pass those problems on in their own communications.

Here are a few examples of how others can impose their beliefs about your ability:

My mom never learned to swim because she KNEW she would sink. The reason she KNEW this was because she had always been told by her father that "she would sink like a rock" if she went into water over her head. Because of repeatedly being told she would sink, she would always stay in the shallow end of the swimming pool. She would only get her feet wet down the shore for summer vacation. She had been conditioned by those who "always told her," and that conditioning stayed with her for the rest of her life.

One damaging event caused me not even to attempt to attend either of my high school proms.

While driving around one night with some friends, one of them dared this girl (whom I held hands with in the school hallways, did our homework together, ate dinners at her house, and with whom I played pick-up baseball, and whom I thought liked me) to kiss me. Her response was something to the effect that she "would rather lick an ashtray than to kiss me." Everyone in the car laughed. I was teased for the next couple of weeks by people who were not even in the car but had heard about what was said to me. Because of that statement, my self-confidence and self-esteem were crushed, so I lacked the courage to ask anyone to any school events or have a girlfriend until after I was out of high school.

As a teacher, I would often have questions during faculty meetings that I was afraid to ask for fear they were "dumb questions." The questions would go unasked in public, and I would usually ask them to a fellow teacher, or they would just go unasked and unanswered.

It is important not to let your own beliefs or the negative statements made by others stop you from enjoying life. Past failures are just that, PAST failures, and are in NO way indicators of future success.

By working on the opportunity pages in this book, you give yourself the gift of knowledge of your past experience but in a way that leads to future success. How do you know what's wrong with a piece of equipment? You take it apart and examine the individual pieces. The opportunity exercises in this book are designed to do just that. They ask you some questions that require you to examine what happened so you can learn from it and improve the outcome for next time.

OPPORTUNITY SECTION:

What missed opportunities have you experienced due to your lack of effective communication skills?

_____

_____

_____

_____

_____

_____

_____

_____

Can you identify the basis for why you missed out? Was it; fear of embarrassment, being told you could not do something, feeling that your response would not be "good enough", etc.?

_____

_____

_____

_____

_____

_____

_____

_____

Based on your answers to the questions above, respond to the following:

Was the opportunity worth missing? Explain.

_____

_____

_____

_____

_____

_____

What is the "worst that could have happened" had you taken advantage of the missed opportunity?

_____

_____

_____

_____

_____

_____

Give at least two examples of how you would have, or could have communicated differently.

_____

_____

_____

_____

_____

_____

MURKY MISUNDERSTANDING

As I started on my quest to achieve a more comprehensive understanding of the communication process, I learned that communication is not taken but given. You are given the opportunity to participate in a communicative setting, and if not taken, then a missed opportunity has occurred. This missed opportunity impacts you, and usually you alone. Others may not understand why you are choosing not to participate, but their conversation will continue with or without you.

Looking at the communication process from this angle made me realize that I needed to start being an active participant. What I should do was start talking more so that people would understand what it was I needed them to hear or do to help me.

This was not an easy process. Great things did not occur immediately, but instead, it was a slow and laborious process. Once I started to communicate with others, my life began to improve. What I found was, when I stopped requiring the other person to figure me out but instead started to communicate my wants and needs, I found a new sense of purpose in my life. Somehow, I had been stuck with a "murky misunderstanding" that communication was only for those who WANTED to communicate instead of for those who *needed* to communicate.

"Communication is a skill that you can learn. It is like riding a bicycle or typing. If you are willing to work at it, you can rapidly improve the quality of every part of your life."

—Brian Tracy

OPPORTUNITY SECTION:

What murky communications have you received that left you puzzled about what was communicated and what your response should be?

_____

_____

_____

_____

_____

_____

What murky communications have you sent to another person that left *them* puzzled about what was communicated and what *their* response should be?

_____

_____

_____

_____

_____

_____

CHAPTER 5:

STOP AVOIDING COMMUNICATION!

"You'll never change your life until you change something you do daily. The secret of success is found in your daily routine."

—John C. Maxwell

As I grew in my understanding of communication, I learned that communicating, in some form, is something humans do every day. This ability to communicate effectively is an essential life skill. Being able to make human connections through the communications process is key to personal and career success. Whether communicating verbally or non-verbally, communication helps provide the opportunity to get our needs and wants met. Through communication, information is gained and then used to learn, solve problems, make decisions, and to more clearly understand each other. Communication helps provide an essential element necessary for achieving all of our goals. Having good communication skills can lead to building new opportunities. I know this sounds easier said than done, but let me tell you about the variety of situations that I and others had placed ourselves in as we took our first steps towards developing better communication skills.

One of the first things that I noticed happening was that I had this inner feeling that I could not continue down the path I was currently traveling. I was not happy (to put it mildly) with my life of being isolated from others. As this inner feeling continued to grow, I decided to make a change.

Deciding that you want to make this change is a very important and necessary step. When you finally realize that you need to change, that is when you can start the change process. Later in the book, we will look at other issues involved in communication as well as examples of different actions you can take to improve your communication skills.

Next, I began to prioritize the parts of the communication process that I wanted to change. For me, the area I thought needed the most immediate attention was my ability to become actively involved, to participate and sustain, the communication process. I was determined to hold up my end of the conversation. Admitting that you need to change is the first step to implementing that change.

I began to realize that in choosing to become more actively involved in the communication process, I was not only letting the other person know that I valued them and what they were trying to relate to me, but also that my responses proved to me that I valued myself and what I wanted to relate mattered, too.

I was taking a chance, a chance that might be awkward at first, but one that could create such a satisfactory result that I would want to keep going. I came to feel more at ease, more focused, and more comfortable if it did not turn out exactly as I had hoped it would. I realized that each attempt was an opportunity for me to learn from the experience and use that knowledge for future attempts.

OPPORTUNITY SECTION:

What is the **main** area in the communication process that is the most difficult for you?

_____

_____

_____

_____

_____

_____

What other areas also cause you to stop communicating?

_____

_____

_____

_____

_____

_____

What steps can you take to improve your communication skills?

_____

_____

_____

_____

_____

_____

_____

THE BLAME GAME—HOW NOT TO PLAY IT!

I have spent some time in this book giving examples of how I felt others had let me down by not doing more to make me part of the conversation. Being told that I had no personality! How I expected them to find out what I wanted and needed. What I failed to realize was that I was giving others the responsibility for my actions.

As stated earlier, part of that came from earlier conditioning of childhood. However, the responsibility issue is a double-edged sword. When I demonstrated behavior either physically, such as "keep away" body language or verbally by remaining silent or only giving one-word answers, I was giving the sender the message that I did not want to communicate, period! "Leave me alone" was my message, whether it was physically conveyed or minimally verbally conveyed, I was not taking a step to engage in the communication.

Fear of being made fun of for my response not being "good enough", or a multitude of other reasons that may have paralyzed me, but it also gave the impression that I couldn't be bothered to answer, or even worse, I was better than the sender was so I did not need to respond to something "beneath me". My silence could have even been interpreted as rudeness; a blank stare often conveys that message. At the same time, I pleaded to be left alone; I was also frustrated that I was alone, only, I was blaming others for it.

We've already talked about the two roles in communication, sender, and receiver. Each is important to the successful outcome of the issue, but you cannot have a successful communication if there are only questions or only responses.

I was expecting others to be responsible for all of the communicating, so it is no wonder people got tired of keeping up both ends of the conversation. In essence, they were only communicating with themselves. I could not expect others to bear the burden of my problem, and I needed to change.

If I wanted people to respect what I communicated, I also needed to respect what they were communicating. By respecting what they communicated, I was also showing them respect, and I had a right to the same in turn. This revelation that I could be an equal in communicating with others made all the difference in the world. I had important things to say just as others did, and we each deserved the respect of the other. Changing others was not something I could do, but I could change myself, and I needed to start right away!

Some actions I needed to change were:

- Focusing on the person speaking
- Repeating something they said back to them for emphasis in my own mind
- Asking them to repeat or rephrase what they had said if I had not heard or understood what they had said.

OPPORTUNITY SECTION:

What actions or phrases will help you become more focused when communicating?

_____

_____

_____

_____

_____

_____

CHAPTER 6:

OLD ME—NEW ME

There are many people who think that communication has the same significance in life as breathing! I, on the other hand, unequivocally and steadfastly hold to the belief that, "If you cannot understand my silence, you cannot understand my words." In fact, there was a poster on my bedroom wall that stated words very similar to that. Although I did not carry this poster around with me, I openly displayed this cavalier attitude about the communication process. This was my constant attitude no matter whom I was communicating with or where I was.

I believed that there was no necessity in sharing my thoughts and feelings with others. Instead, it was my mindset that people should be able to read my mind or understand my comments, thus figuring out what it was that I needed and wanted. It was this communication mindset that would cause me and others many years of grief, misunderstanding, and struggles. I was willing to communicate with anyone who was able to understand my communication mindset, but there was no one. So be it! Life went on! Unfortunately, life went on without me.

After years of maintaining this communication mindset, I realized that YES, life would go on for those who could communicate effectively, and I was leaving myself out of life. For me, this lack of any social interaction seemed to affirm my belief that communicating with others was not something that I was capable of achieving.

These numerous less-than-successful communication interactions were validation for me that the communication process was both unachievable and insurmountable. Instead of continuing to arrange for more opportunities to communicate, I instead chose to further seclude myself from others. When a chance for communication with others did arise, I would retreat to another room, ignore the person, develop an imaginary illness, or invent some excuse to avoid interaction.

At family gatherings, when I would retreat to another room or ignore someone who was trying to initiate a conversation with me, I would repeatedly hear my mom and other adults saying, "There goes Billy separating himself again from the rest of the family", "I wish he would stop being so anti-social", "If he would only stop isolating himself, he would be much better off", "People would talk to him if he only gave them the chance."

The reasons I chose to separate myself from others, often by just sitting alone or just going somewhere to be alone, meant I did not have to interact with anyone, and I was actively choosing to do this as a defense mechanism. These actions did not solve my problem; instead, they were only a temporary fix to an uncomfortable situation.

Another method I used to avoid interaction with others was my continuous imaginary "illnesses" just before the school bus would arrive or just before physical education class. These "illnesses" would last just long enough for me to avoid having to do something that I dreaded (i.e., going to school or participating in gym class). Occasionally, my mom or dad would comment about how much better I looked and acted once the school bus had passed our house. The school nurse also questioned how such "severe symptoms" would disappear in time for me to report to my next class following gym class, or how they would only occur on certain days of the week. Once she figured out what the problem really was, she would often allow me to be her aide during gym class.

On the rare occasion when I did choose to remain in close proximity to others, I would stand with my arms crossed, have a scowl look on my face, not make eye contact, or openly show signs of non-interest (non-verbal body language) no matter what the topic of discussion. Although these contemptuous actions, on my part, were "clearly" intended to send the message "leave me alone," others in the room would still attempt to draw me into their conversation. It was not until later on in life that I would become aware that my non-verbal body language was, in fact, creating a physical barrier to effective communication between myself and others.

Looking back on my life, this "leave me alone/avoidance method" did not serve me well. This included a limited dad-daughter relationship, two failed marriages where I was repeatedly told that I "lacked the ability to communicate my wants or needs or that this behavior allowed me to ignore an issue for fear of having to "talk about it." I had an absolute dread of having to attend social gatherings, and the list goes on and on. This philosophy also followed me into the work environment where, due to my limited ability to actively participate in successful interactive communications with others during office meetings, my superintendent wrote as an improvement goal on several of my yearly performance reports, "Dr. Lane needs to participate more during administrative meetings."

Based on these examples, and among others, I have written this book to assist those who have or had a similar philosophy/behavior that they want or need to change! For those choosing to continue isolating themselves from others, having limited or no communicative interaction with others and/or continuing to make yourself appear unapproachable, I can guarantee that other people will continue to leave you alone! How do I know, I speak from experience!

"Let me tell you this: if you meet a loner, no matter what they tell you, it's not because they enjoy solitude. It's because they have tried to blend into the world before, and people continue to disappoint them."

—Jodi Picoult, *My Sister's Keeper*

OPPORTUNITY SECTION:

List ways you chose to isolate yourself from communicating with others.

_____

_____

_____

_____

_____

_____

What positive steps can you take to open the communication process as both a sender and receiver?

_____

_____

_____

_____

_____

_____

What benefits do you expect to see happen as a result of these changes?

_____

_____

_____

_____

_____

_____

CHAPTER 7:

OLD NAVY V. NEW NAVY

When I doubted my communication skills, the acronym NAVY stood for Never Again Volunteer Yourself. At meetings or conferences, I was the last one to volunteer for anything. If the assignment asked for a volunteer, I would close my eyes relying on the childhood misnomer that "if I cannot see them, then they cannot see me." Sometimes, rather than close my eyes, I would take an immediate interest in my shoes and the need for them to be re-tied. I have noticed that this practice is one that others will sometimes use in uncomfortable situations. These practices have worked well for me and others because very seldom were we chosen!

As my communication skills began to improve, the acronym took on a totally different meaning for me. NAVY now meant Never Avoid Volunteering Yourself. Whenever possible, I was quick to raise my hand when a volunteer was needed. When working in small groups, I would volunteer to be the writer, note taker, the idea collector, etc.

During my presentations or workshops, I always provide an opportunity for a volunteer to come on stage and assist me. After the activity is over, the volunteer is given a t-shirt, coffee cup, or some other token of gratitude. It is not difficult to notice, what I perceive to be, a look of disappointment from others in the audience who now wished they had volunteered.

Example: During a recent presentation to the state FFA presidents, I asked for a volunteer, and after helping, she received a Superman t-shirt. I overheard one of the other presidents say, "Ah, man, I should have volunteered!"

Is volunteering scary? You bet it is! Whenever you put yourself in front of others, you are opening yourself up to both negative and positive results. Do I regret the times I have volunteered myself? Let me tell you; there have been more positives times than negative ones!

Example: I volunteered to work on a political campaign. This led to other volunteer work on other candidate's campaigns. As I grew in my political expertise, I became a paid employee and had the opportunity to meet two presidents and have a signed picture on my desk from a former vice-president.

OPPORTUNITY SECTION:

List the actions you will take to make yourself volunteer more.

_____

_____

_____

_____

_____

_____

When I doubted my ability to be an effective communicator, I lived by the thought that NAVY stood for *never again volunteer yourself.* If I were at a meeting and they would ask for a volunteer to come up and participate in an activity, I closed my eyes and hoped that they would not call on me. Using the childish belief that, "If I could not see them, then they could not see me."

As I have gained confidence in my ability to communicate effectively, I started believing that NAVY stood for *now actively volunteer yourself.* This approach has brought with it self-confidence and often has served as a conversation starter.

Example: I was asked to serve as a judge at a local competition. It was decided that rather than have each judge provide a question to the contestants, one judge would ask everyone's questions. Notes would be provided to this judge to ask, thus reducing having the contestant wonder whom would be asking the next question. I immediately volunteered and questions were handed to me and I provided a few of my own. After the competition, as I was walking around waiting for the results, a few people approached me and told me how thought provoking my questions were.

Example: During a majority of my speaking engagements or presentations I will ask for a volunteer to join me and help with the demonstration of a point I am trying to make. This volunteer is rewarded with a coffee cup, beach ball, or a t-shirt for their volunteering. When they leave the stage, I can see the look of frustration on many of the other attendees' faces because they wish they had been willing to volunteer.

OPPORTUNITY SECTION:

Which navy are you part of? Provide three examples.

_____

_____

_____

_____

_____

_____

What changes are you prepared to make the next time you have the opportunity to volunteer?

_____

_____

_____

_____

_____

_____

CHAPTER 8:

MAKING YOUR COMMUNICATION EFFECTIVE

"If you just communicate, you can get by. But if you communicate skillfully, you can work miracles."

—Jim Rohn

"The quality of your life is the quality of your communication."

—Tony Robbins

"Communication is more of an art than a science. There is no right or wrong way to communicate, and each person must develop his/her own style of communication. Communication must be HOT. That means HONEST, OPEN, and TWO-WAY."

—Dan Oswald

There are two parts that make up the communication process: the sending and receiving of information. Having better communication skills requires improving the process for both how we send and how we receive messages. This two-way process occurs when the receiver understands and receives the message in the manner intended by the sender. For me, communication was a one-way process, someone else did the communicating, and I chose whether I wanted to receive or respond to their message. This approach to communication caused a litany of issues for me and anyone wanting to communicate with me.

I eventually learned that during the communication process, both a speaker and a receiver are required to participate. This participation requires that each perform role reversal. Role reversal means that sometimes you are the speaker (message sender) and sometimes you are the listener (message receiver). What is important is that role reversal frequently occurs during communication. Having effective communication skills involves improving both how we send and how we receive messages. Effective communication can be learned and improved upon anytime in an individual's life. By becoming a more skilled communicator, your ability to connect with people will greatly improve.

Effective communication means not only the quality of your words but also the quantity of words. Could you say what you have to say in one paragraph versus three? Just because you have used lots of words, doesn't mean that it's better, only longer. We have all known people who just love to hear themselves talk; they could talk all day! Listening to that, however, is something that most people would avoid at all costs.

In Chapter 1, we learned about Tiffany Southwell, the teacher whose students voluntarily gave up the use of their phones and wrote about their experience during that time. She noted that some students could not last even a few minutes without checking their phone. They were not expecting a message, there was no "alert chime" to let them know they had received a message, but they had to check. I wonder how much of what they received really mattered, or is it just a tidal wave of information? Effective communication is also efficient communication.

Are you wasting time putting out too much information, essentially boring your audience with "filler info"?

Another issue with effective communication, especially with social media, is that not only are people sharing too much information as far as quantity is concerned, but they are also sharing too much information of a personal nature.

Other than your family members and your healthcare practitioners, the world does not need to know the results of your medical tests or procedures, the details of your break up, or other highly personal messages that really should be left to a personal message rather than a social media post. Social media sites are out there for the world to see; even if you have just posted something to your friends, it may be much more than they want to learn publicly. People also tire of the drama; when everything is over-the-top dramatic, it loses its effectiveness.

MUST AND WANT!

In order to improve your communication skills, there needs to be a recognition that a change MUST occur and that there is a strong WANT inside of you to make the change. The important word in that sentence is YOU! Without realizing the importance of both of these factors, improving your communication skills will be difficult. Some people have their "AHA" moment for only one of these. To successfully improve one's communication skills, both the must and the want have to be there. Others may have tried to change you by helping you, telling you how to, or even demanded that you change.

As a way to help you, they may have provided ideas for change, enrolled you in training sessions, and even told you how nice it would be if you changed. The problem with them telling or trying to help you change was that they were the ones trying to make you change, not you wanting to change! Since you had little interest, there was no desire on your part to make the change. There may have been times that you wanted to change, but either did not know how or felt the change would be too difficult. Improvement in your communication skills will not occur until YOU accept that there must be a change and YOU want this change to happen. Let your communication skills evolve at a pace you are comfortable with. You do not need to change them all at once.

Example: My "must and want" moments both came at the same time when I finally realized that I must improve two of my communication skills. First, I must become a better listener because it seemed that during every conversation my mind would wander. During a conversation, someone would be talking about their dog and the next thing I knew, my dog, Meniscus, became the focus of my thoughts. These thoughts included; had I remembered to feed her, did she have fresh water, would she be OK until I got home to go out for her walk. Instead of listening to the speaker, a single trigger word would cause me to drift off somewhere far away from the conversation.

OPPORTUNITY SECTION:

Why **MUST** your communication skills improve?

_____

_____

_____

_____

_____

Why do you **WANT** to improve your communication skills?

_____

_____

_____

_____

_____

CHAPTER 9:

TAKE YOUR TIME—START SMALL

Change can and will be difficult. There is a saying that the only person who likes change is a baby with a soiled diaper. Having listed the must and want reasons for changing your communication skills, the next step is determining how. Have you ever heard the question, "How do you eat an elephant?" The answer is "One spoonful at a time." This is not meant to be funny. It is wise advice when attempting to do something different or difficult. All new endeavors require a slow and careful approach. When I decided to improve my communication skills, I chose to compile a strategy. The strategy I chose was to start working with a small number of people in safe and controlled situations and only work on one communication difficulty at a time.

From previous experiences, I know I was more comfortable and successful in having individual one-on-one communications with just one person than with a group of people. Often, when I was in a large group setting, there were too many distractions keeping me from being able to follow along or participate. When in these settings, I found myself becoming self-conscious and often felt unnecessary anxiety about my communication attempts. Many times, I felt that when in large group settings, I felt that my attempts at communication were less than successful.

As I thought back on these less than successful communications, they seemed to occur when someone else would start the communication process. In these situations, I would become nervous, stumble with my words and, finally, not be able to speak at all. I hoped that working with individuals would provide me the opportunity to participate in the communication process in a more relaxed and controlled situation where I would have an opportunity to carefully listen and participate.

The ideal part of these one-on-one communication situations was that I could sometimes manage to be the initiator of the communication. Initiating the communication provided me the chance to be prepared with what I wanted to say. Having my thoughts prepared ahead of time about what I wanted to communicate with others allowed me to feel more confident. As I became more confident, I noticed that my attempts at communication were more frequent and longer lasting. As I communicated on a more frequent basis with others, I found the need for preparing my thoughts ahead of time diminish. That is not to say that I no longer thought about a variety of topics I might want to discuss beforehand, but not every communication required me to prepare ahead of time.

See the section *MORE THAN A ONE SUBJECT SPEAKER* for ideas on a variety of subjects to use when attempting to start the communication process.

It is important to remember that you need to practice these one-on-one communication opportunities at a pace that makes you feel comfortable. Once I started communicating with people, I noticed that individual communication opportunities were all around me. You never know what you are missing until you attempt to see something from a different perspective. These individualized settings provided the confidence and success I needed to eventually progress to communicate with larger groups of people. Below are some examples of situations where and how I chose to practice communicating with individuals or small groups.

The group of people I first started my attempts at communicating with were service people. My definition of service people is those who provide others with a needed service and are getting paid to do so. For me, these service people included; the greeter at Walmart™, the cashier at the grocery store, the tellers at the bank, waitresses, and waiters, and people at the local drug store. As a majority of these places are ones I frequent on a daily or weekly basis, I found it easier to start here.

This is how I started: When I was in a store, I would speak to the person about how crowded the store was or the lack of customers. I would also notice if an employee was new to the store and involve them in a discussion about how long they had been working at the store. One employee told me this was his first day at the store and I complimented him on the "wonderful job" he was doing and how I was sure he would be successful.

Another place I would try to start communications was with clerks at my local drug store. I have been a regular customer at this drug store, so, on most occasions, when I walked in the front door, I was greeted with, "Good Morning, Dr. Lane. How are you today?" After exchanging pleasantries, I would often, in jest, mention to the clerks that maybe I should get a job working there since I was at the store more often than they were. This would lead to laughs and brief communication exchanges depending on how busy everyone was.

Previously, when in restaurants, I would order my food by pointing to the item on the menu, mumbling something unintelligible and thanking the server, with as few words as necessary when the meal was delivered. Now, when ordering my food, I will discuss with the waitress or waiter what the specials of the day are and which meal they would recommend. When it appeared that my server had an opportunity to talk, I would discuss how good the service was and ask them how they liked working at the restaurant.

Usually, these communication exchanges lasted only a few seconds, but through them, I was gaining the confidence to speak with people whom I do not know. As I became more confident in my ability to successfully communicate with others, I would ask if I could speak to the manager and provide the manager compliments about how good my server had been.

Being a volunteer is another way that can be used to help improve your communication interaction within a small group setting. One of my friends even volunteers at his church, helping to park cars before Sunday church services. Since he can help provide the parishioners with a need, the social interaction and communication is in a less stressful and relaxed setting.

People are generally more willing to interact with those who are providing them with something they need or those making stressful conditions more comfortable.

Example: When I enter a store, I will hold the door for the person behind me and let them enter first. Despite the look on their face, most of them will respond with, "Thank You." I will respond, "You're welcome and have a nice day." Sometimes this will lead to further conversation, but if it did not, I still reflect on the encounter as a success because I have spoken to someone and they responded.

As I have grown more confident in my communications with others, on occasion, I will hold the door at a restaurant for other people and say to them, "Welcome to (name of the restaurant) and I hope you enjoy your meal." People are often surprised when, a few minutes later, they see me standing in line behind them waiting to be seated.

Another way I have practiced my communication skills is to walk into a store and ask for directions to a specific item. Before one of my trips, I needed travel bags to store my clothes. When I entered the store, I found a store employee and asked him where the clothing storage bags would be found. He started giving me directions and then realized that he was getting lost just giving me directions, so he offered to walk with me to the item's location. Along the way, we talked about where I was traveling, and I asked him about his day and the upcoming bad weather they were predicting. Clothing bags found and a successful communication attempt!

OPPORTUNITY SECTION:

List three methods you plan to use in order to improve the quality of your communication.

_____

_____

_____

_____

_____

_____

NOTICE WHAT OTHERS LIKE

Sometimes I would find it difficult to speak with people, even those people whom I know well. For me, this included family members, co-workers, and even my best friends. It seemed that when I was speaking with them, finding new areas for communication was difficult. Whenever we would have a conversation, it seemed like all the good topics had already been talked about way too much, and no one wanted to talk about them anymore. This often caused me to have little to talk to them about and, therefore, would choose to isolate myself from everyone. After realizing that this was not the way I wanted to live my life, I needed to figure out a solution to this problem.

What I did that helped me have conversations with others was noticing what it was that they liked. Starting or having a more in-depth communication with other people sometimes requires you to notice what their interests are, or what they most like to talk about. After repeatedly observing effective communicators, I became more aware of how they would pick up and start conversations that focused on other peoples' interests. Once I started communicating about what others had an interest in, my conversational abilities improved immensely. The problem was that as my conversational group grew, it was difficult to keep track of their particular interests.

One technique that I found that helped solve this problem was to either mentally envision or write down topics or the person's likes that they talked about on a regular basis. I developed a list of each person's likes/interests along with a list of "conversation starter questions." It then became my job to listen to others talk and find out what interested them and then use these topics as a basis for my conversations with them. This allowed me, when the opportunity arose, to have a list of their likes or their interests that we could talk about.

Example: My grandmother liked to talk about her family. This became the topic I would use to talk to her about when we had the opportunity. I would ask her questions about her sisters, her parents, if she remembered her grandparents, what her life was like when she was growing up, etc.

Example: One of my best friends likes to talk about baseball. Whenever we talk, it is inevitable that the conversation will quickly drift to the baseball team both of us like. I try to keep up with the latest trades, injuries, game results, etc. so that when we talk, this information is something I can use to extend our conversations.

This chart provides some examples of people, their likes/interests, and conversation starter questions.

Person	Likes/ Interests	Conversation Starter Questions
Mother	Cooking	"What are you cooking for dinner?" "Do you have any favorite meals you like to prepare?" "Which meals do you like to make for your friends?" "Have you ever cooked a meal that nobody liked?" "What did you do?" "What is your signature dish?" "What is your 'go-to' dish?" "Are there any meals you would like to cook but think we may not like them?
Dad	Sports	"Why do you like ____?" "What makes them your favorite?" "Have you ever been to a _____ game?" "Have you ever seen _____ play in person?" "What do you think are _____ chances of making the playoffs?" "Who is your favorite player?"
Sister	Boyfriend	"Does _____ have a job?" "How did you and _____ meet?" "Who are his family members?" "What sports does he like to play?" "Does he have any pets?" "Are you in any school/college classes together?" "What is his favorite ice cream flavor?"
Brother	School	"Who is your favorite teacher?" "What is your favorite subject in school?" "Are any of your friends in your classes?"

Grandparents	"Good old days"	"What was it like when you were my age?" "What are some things that are different now than when you were growing up?" "What major changes have occurred and do you like them?" "Do you think you would like to be growing up now?"
Neighbors	Children, pets, house	"How are your children doing?" "Who does your yard work?" "How was your vacation?" "Do you have any plans for your next vacation?" "Who takes care of your pet(s) when you are away?" "Do you like my new _____?"

OPPORTUNITY SECTION:

Complete your own chart to help you improve your communication with others.

Person	Likes/ Interests	Conversation Subject Starters

COMMUNICATION IS SIMILAR TO WRITING A LETTER

When communicating, I recommend that you remember this: Good communication is like writing a letter (e-mails, for those of you under twenty). Each of the following components plays an important part in good communication:

Greeting/Opening Statement/Question:

When both communicating and writing, begin with a greeting/ opening statement/question. People have their own "issues" and may be reluctant to assume more by entering into a conversation that they feel is irrelevant to them. They may have other things on their mind, or they may not think you are addressing them, so the use of a good greeting/opening statement/question will help "catch their attention." https://zoom.us/j/8315244949 Catching someone's attention allows for the possibility that they will be intrigued enough to want to talk with you or read further.

Examples: "Hi", "Hello", "Good Morning", "To Whom It May Concern", "Dear Customer", "It sure is a nice day." "I cannot wait until this weekend!" "How are you?" "Have you been waiting long for the bus?" "Do you think we will get all that snow/rain/heat like the weather people are saying we are expected to get this weekend?"

Staying On Topic:

Whether you are writing and speaking, you should have a body of information. In writing, remember how each paragraph contains a specific topic. When having a conversation, it is IMPORTANT to stay on the topic being discussed. When speaking, it is important that you limit your communication to one or two closely related topics. This makes the information you are sharing or receiving easier to follow. The person with whom you are speaking can follow along without becoming distracted, and when listening, you know which topic to focus on. As the speaker, "staying on topic" allows the listener to follow along with one or two topics of discussion. This also allows the listener to respond with follow-up questions, ask for more details or provide comments. When a speaker talks about many topics or the conversation seems to have no "sense of direction," the listener will soon be looking for a way to exit the conversation.

Here's an example of a conversation containing too may topics:

"I went to a really good movie last night!", "Have you seen the new Star Wars movie yet?" "Last weekend we visited the city where my grandfather was born and saw a big mountain with snow on top." "It was so exciting because we got to fly on an airplane!"

Example of a conversation that contains one topic:

Speaker (S) "Yesterday was my mom's birthday, and we surprised her with dinner at home."

Listener (L) "What did you make her for dinner?"

(S) "We made spaghetti which is her favorite meal."

(L) "Did you have meatballs with the spaghetti?"

(S) "Yes, my mom really likes turkey meatballs."

(L) "Did you have a birthday cake for her also?"

(S) "Yes, we had a chocolate cake, and mom only let us put two candles on it because she said if we put a candle for each birthday, we would probably set the house fire alarm off!"

(L) "Your mom has a good sense of humor and sure sounds like she had a really good birthday."

(S) "She said it was her best birthday ever!"

Ending/Departing Statement:

When writing or speaking, having an ending or a departing statement is essential. Both your written communication and your conversation should have some type of ending or departing statement. Without some form of ending, both the person with whom you are talking or the listener will wonder what to do next. With the conversation coming to an unspecific end, both the speaker and the listener are put into uncomfortable positions.

The speaker may be waiting for the listener to respond or might just be pausing to collect their thoughts, etc. At the same time, the listener is wondering what to say to keep the conversation going. Whether it is the speaker or the listener, the choosing of an ending or a departing statement not only signals the end of this conversation, but also allows for the possibility of future discussion or a termination of the conversation.

Examples of a conversation lacking an ending/departing comment:

Recently, while attending a social event, I was talking to a person, and the conversation was going along well. It was a successful back and forth exchange of ideas and topics. We talked for about ten minutes, and while I was in the middle of discussing something, he just turned around and walked away. He had asked me a question, so I know it was something he wanted to know about, but how he chose to end the conversation left me wondering.

Where I used to live in Japan, I had a neighbor who always wanted to talk to me. We would talk for about five minutes and then when he finished saying something, even if we were in the middle of a lengthy conversation, he would just walk away. This happened every time we talked. Because there was never a closing or departing statement, I always wondered if I had said something wrong that offended him.

Here are some examples of appropriate ending/departing comments:

"We should talk more about this after the session."

"Would you like to go over to the coffee shop across the street and continue this conversation?"

"It was nice talking to you. Have a nice day."

"It is time for me to get ready to catch the bus. Goodbye!"

Example: After speaking at the Autism World Festival in Vancouver, Canada, I was approached by one of my workshop attendees who asked if I had time to talk to him in more detail about my presentation. We talked for about twenty minutes when he stated, "Dr. Lane, I really have enjoyed talking with you, and I hope we can talk more about this. Would you mind if my wife and I joined you at your dinner table to further continue the discussion?"

OPPORTUNITY SECTION:

In your own words, discuss how communication is similar to writing a letter.

_____

_____

_____

_____

_____

_____

CONVEYING YOUR MESSAGE—The 5 C's

For me, when I finally started communicating on a more regular basis with others, I found the circumstances most comfortable when the conversation was free-flowing. The best way I have found for keeping the communication process moving was to remember that a conversation is much like writing a letter. Whether you are writing a letter or speaking to someone, the purpose of your communication is to convey a message. Remember these "five C's" in your communication:

The Five C's are: Clear, Complete, Consistent, Correct, and Courteous.

Listed below are discussions and examples that will demonstrate how each of these "five C's" have helped me in the communication process.

CLEAR—During communication, it is important to keep "on topic," and use the exact words to clearly state your message's intent. Staying on topic means that, if the conversation is pertaining to the planets that are visible in the sky tonight, your questions or responses should be related to that topic. Be sure to state the topic you are speaking about early and often. This will ensure that whoever hears your message knows exactly the topic you are discussing.

Your use of appropriate questions or responses to the conversation will help to advance and prolong the conversation. Communicating more clearly will increase the likelihood of achieving your desired outcome.

I have found that by advancing the conversation, people will stay engaged for longer and are more willing to talk with you now and in the future. When the sender (speaker) or receiver (listener) goes off topic, the tendency is for the conversation to be shortened or the conversation ends awkwardly, and this may cause people to be less willing to converse with you should future opportunities occur.

Staying on topic is paramount to carrying on a lengthy and interesting conversation. As you read the example below, notice how going off topic quickly puts an end to this conversation.

Example of going off topic:

Recently, I was talking to a friend about the flowers she had just planted in her backyard when our neighbor came over and joined the conversation. His first statement was that he had received a letter from a friend he had not heard from in a long time. We both smiled and said we hoped the letter contained good news. His next statement was that what was more important about the letter was that it contained some stamps he had never seen before. Trying to return to our original conversation about the newly planted flowers was quickly halted when his third statement was about some budget projections he had made and was planning to present them at the next Homeowners Association meeting on Thursday. My friend and I politely excused ourselves from the conversation, and the next time we talked, it was in a location that was not visible for our neighbor to see us.

Example of staying on topic:

During lunch with my friends in Florida, we were discussing the cold weather. I shared that having left Baltimore Washington Airport the previous day with three inches of snow on the ground and the wind chill factor about ten degrees, the weather in Florida was a pleasant change. After sharing this information with my friends, we all glanced around the restaurant and started discussing the variety of clothing that people were wearing. I spoke about a lady I saw entering the restaurant who was wearing boots and a long winter jacket. One of my friends looked out on the porch area and saw someone who had to be from a cold weather climate who was wearing shorts and a t-shirt. My other friend said she had noticed a lady walking her dog around the neighborhood wearing a blanket on top of her clothing. We all shared a chuckle about the various outfits we had seen recently and how everyone had their unique manner for adjusting to the Florida weather. For the next ten minutes, until lunch arrived, our discussion was totally centered on one topic.

COMPLETE—In oral communication, it is important that you express your idea completely to minimize the chance of the receiver misunderstanding what it is you are trying to express. Sometimes when we are speaking about a subject that may make us feel uncomfortable or we are not sure how the other person feels about the subject, we tend to withhold information or not address the topic. Examples of these subjects are; money, dating, religion, and politics.

Example of incomplete communication:

You notice a particular girl has been visiting the place you work on a regular basis. You think she is pretty and decide you want to ask her to go to the movies with you this weekend. One day when she enters, it is time for your break, so you walk over to her and introduce yourself. She tells you her name, and the two of you begin talking. You notice that your break is just about over,

so you stand up and tell her you need to get back to work. You both say goodbye, and you return to work. You begin to notice that she is no longer coming into your work and you realize you missed your opportunity to ask her to the movies because your communications with her were incomplete. What you wanted to say was left unsaid.

Example of complete communication:

You notice a particular girl has been visiting the place you work on a regular basis. You think she is pretty and you decide you want to ask her to go to the movies with you this weekend. One day when she enters, it is time for your break, so you walk over to her and introduce yourself. She tells you her name, and the two of you begin talking. You notice that your break is just about over, so you stand up and tell her you need to get back to work. Before returning to work, you mention to her that there is a movie showing in your local theater you would like to see and ask if she would like to go with you. After her reply, you both say goodbye and you return to work. What you wanted to communicate to her was expressed.

CONSISTENT—When orally communicating, assume the listener has a limited amount of time to completely understand your communication. Your communication with others should be free-flowing, with active participation by both parties and should not drag on and on. There is no need to say in many words what can be said in fewer words. Generally, it is best to get to the point as quickly as possible.

Example of inconsistent communication:

You have decided to talk to a friend about a behavior of his that really bothers many of your mutual friends. _____ has this habit of chewing his food with his mouth open, and now many of his friends are refusing to dine with him. Since you are his best friend, you volunteered to address the subject with him. You and _____ are sitting in a restaurant, and you notice that tonight his behavior is worse than ever. People from other tables are glancing over and making rude comments about his eating behaviors. When he puts down his fork, you ask him if you two could speak for a minute before he resumes eating. He agrees, so you ask him if he knows what you want to talk to him about. He says he has no idea and asks if there is a problem. You ask if he has noticed how many of the people in the restaurant keep glancing over at him while he is eating. He looks surprised and says he had not noticed. He suggests that maybe they are just admiring his new haircut. Your look of disapproval clearly indicates that is not the reason, but you are not sure what else to say so the meal resumes without the problem being addressed.

Example of concise communication:

You have decided to speak to a friend about a behavior that really bothers many of your mutual friends. This person has a habit of chewing his food with his mouth open and now many of his friends are refusing to dine with him. Since you are his best friend, you volunteered to address the subject with him. You are both sitting in a restaurant and you notice that tonight his behavior appears to be worse than ever. People from other tables are glancing over and making snide comments about his eating behaviors. When he puts down his fork, you ask him if you could speak to him for a minute before he resumes eating. He agrees, so you ask him if he knows what you want to talk to him about.

He says he has no idea and asks if there is a problem. You ask if he has noticed how many of the people in the restaurant keep glancing over at him while he is eating. He looks surprised and says he had not noticed. He suggests that maybe everyone is just admiring his new haircut. You smile at his attempt at humor but begin discussing the problem and the impact this behavior is having not only on the other diners, but also on many of his friends.

CORRECT—When using oral communication, make sure that your words are being used correctly and the person to whom you are speaking is addressed in the correct manner. On many occasions, people are judged by the way they speak and address others. This is something that should be remembered in all social or business settings. The use of words incorrectly or failing to address someone with the respect they deserve can impact how others perceive you.

Example of incorrect communication:

On the first day at your new job, you are introduced to the boss of the company. During the introduction, she is introduced as Dr. Shelby Smith. If you said, "It be nice to meet you this after day, Shelby", your response would not create a good first impression not only because of your incorrect use of correct language skills, but also for not addressing the person with whom you are speaking in the correct manner.

Example of correct communication:

On the first day at your new job, you are introduced to the boss of the company. During the introduction, she is introduced as Dr. Shelby Smith. If you said, "Dr. Smith, it is a pleasure to meet you today", your response would be a good first impression of your correct use of language skills and probably would leave her impressed that you addressed her in the correct manner.

COURTEOUS—Make sure that you have included all pertinent information in your oral communication. The inclusion of all the pertinent information will allow the receiver to more easily understand what you are saying and not have to read what is on your mind. It is important that the receiver of your message not be left guessing about your thoughts and ideas.

By failing to provide the receiver of your message with details, they become unsure how to respond. They may not want to make an uninformed decision, and most of the time will respond negatively to your invitation or request.

Example of being courteously incorrect:

You say to someone at work, "How about joining a group of us after work?" The receiver of your message is left with many unanswered questions. These may include: what are you planning to do, where are you planning to go, how long do you intend to stay, who else is planning on going, have I dressed appropriately for this unknown place, what do I need to bring, and the list goes on. When you withhold details about what you are discussing to the receiver of your message, you are being discourteous.

Example of being courteously correct:

You say to someone at work, "How about joining a group of us after work?" "All the guys from floor five are planning to go over to Bob's house for some pizza and soda." "Since Bob and his wife are going out to see a movie at seven, we will only be there for a couple of hours, and since everyone is going there right from work, everyone will be wearing their uniforms." "Bob says anyone who wants to show up should bring a bottle of soda." With many of the details about your invitation or request provided, the receiver of your message is better able to make an informed decision.

Before beginning the journey to improve my communication skills, the manner I preferred to use to communicate with others was to write them a letter. When I chose to express my needs and wants through letter writing, I found that using the five C's was a helpful method. When people would receive a note explaining the issue/problem, they would generally continue the communication process. At that time, I did not know any other way of communicating effectively.

Although I do not recommend constantly using written communications, as a starting point, I often found it to be effective. Hopefully, as you work through this book, you will improve your communication to a point where you can address an issue/situation through conversation.

OPPORTUNITY SECTION:

List and briefly describe the five c's.

_____

_____

_____

_____

_____

_____

_____

_____

_____

_____

_____

_____

_____

_____

_____

_____

_____

_____

_____

_____

_____

_____

_____

TRANSFERRING THE INFORMATION

Communication is the transferring of information. The important part of this previous statement is to understand how this process is accomplished.

Transferring of information is done through the use of verbal, non-verbal, or written methods. Verbal communication can be further divided into oral communication and written communication.

Verbal communication is when sounds and language are used to convey a message between individuals by using speech. Conversations between friends, announcements, presentations, and speeches are all forms of verbal communication. Through the use of spoken language, most people convey their expression of beliefs, emotions, feelings, ideas, and thoughts. Verbal communication can consist of one person speaking to another, one person speaking to many people, and many people speaking to many people. This form of communication is used by the majority of people as their primary means of communicating. When using verbal communication, remember that the receiver of your message may have their own beliefs, emotions, feelings, ideas, and thoughts on the topic, thus causing barriers in the delivery and receiving of the message. When the matter under discussion is temporary or direct interaction is required, use verbal communication. The use of verbal communication can build rapport and trust.

There are both advantages and disadvantages when using verbal communication. The advantages of using verbal communication are that the speaker is provided with swift feedback, and based on non-verbal cues, a determination can be made on the truthfulness of what is being said. The disadvantages of using verbal communication are that limited time is provided for deep thought before one speaks, therefore, once a statement is made, it is very difficult to retract, and sometimes the message is misinterpreted. (See section "Be Careful What You Post" for more of an explanation.)

Written communication is the use of written signs, words, or symbols to convey a message. When words are properly written, they can be read and easily understood. Written communication is a formal and less flexible method of communication. When using written communication, it is important that the message "cuts through the clutter." This can be accomplished by having a message that is clear, focused, confident, and relevant. The message should contain a beginning, middle, and end. Make sure the words chosen adapt to the intended audience of the message.

Just as with oral communication, there are both advantages and disadvantages of written communication. The advantages of using written communication are that the writer is provided time for the message to be carefully thought out, and revised and edited before being sent. The disadvantages of using written communication are that the writer does not receive immediate feedback, more time is required to compose a written message, and people may have difficulty writing effectively. Written communication plays a large part in the business world as evidenced by the amount of paperwork involved (memos, forms, spreadsheets, data charts, etc.).

Non-verbal communication is "communicating without words". In other words, any communication that is not oral or written.

Non-verbal communication often occurs unconsciously and speaks volumes about our "real" feelings, thoughts, and desires. When a speaker's verbal and non-verbal messages conflict, the receiver of the message instantly relies on the non-verbal cues. A person's non-verbal communication is more honest than their words. This provides the significance of the saying "Actions speak louder than words", because non-verbal messages often occur unconsciously and are difficult to control.

COMMUNICATION—ACTIVE, NOT PASSIVE

In order for communication to be successful, each person must be involved. Communication is a two-way process, meaning that each person should talk for half of the time they are participating in a conversation. This means that the opportunity to speak should be roughly a (fifty-fifty) split. At different times during the conversation, each participant will sometimes be the speaker and will sometimes be the listener. There are some people, and we all know at least one, who like to speak more than they like to listen. This does not mean that communication cannot occur if only one person is doing the talking, as long as the other person has been given an opportunity to speak and make their point.

If you find yourself in a conversation where a person is monopolizing the conversation, remember there is nothing passive about the listening process. It is your responsibility as the listener to be engaged at the same level of the communication process as the speaker. It is important that, as the listener, you take a more active role in the conversation. Being an active listener means you are fully involved in the conversation. Active listening is a sign of respect to the speaker. By not becoming a participant in the conversation, what could happen is that the speaker will realize they are the only one actively participating and the communications between you both may become reduced or even non-existent.

Example: I have a friend that everyone who knows her says that "she can speak to a blade of grass!' She has the ability to start a conversation with anyone or almost anything and talk MOST of the time. I have learned that the only way for me to be the speaker is to take an active role in the conversation process. I do this through the use of open-ended questions that help me clarify what she was talking about to make sure I have received her message accurately and by providing her feedback on what she was talking about. Some examples I have used to assume a more active role in our conversations are: "That was a good point you made about the rug in the dining room." "Do you think that the issue at work will ever change as long as that person is in charge?" "Would you mind talking more about the new car you are planning to purchase?"

OPPORTUNITY SECTION:

List your ideas for becoming a more active listener.

_____

_____

_____

_____

_____

_____

PPP BECAUSE PMP…PMP

"Nothing is stronger than habit."
—Ovid Ars Amatoria

"Persistence gives confidence, there is no good or bad, but thinking makes it so."
—Shakespeare

"Practice makes perfect."
—Latin proverb

Practice, perform, and practice again because practice makes perfect and continued practice makes permanent. This was something that I remember hearing the head football coach say to the team during practice. He would say to the players that unless they were doing numerous repetitions of their blocking skills, their ball-handling skills, or their pass coverage assignments, then what we as coaches were teaching them would be forgotten.

Whenever the players would complain about having to do the same drill over and over again, the coach would say "PMP PMP." The players would respond loudly "Practice makes perfect and continued practice makes permanent" and the drill would continue.

I began to notice an improvement in my communication skills after I started the practice-perform-reflect process. During this process, I would repeatedly practice a particular communication skill. Sometimes I would practice this skill in front of a mirror, with my dog, or while I was walking alone around the block. Practice-practice-practice. Soon, I got tired of practicing and thought it was time to apply the skill.

After I applied the skill, I would reflect on how successful or less than successful my attempt had been. Answering the questions below helped me determine whether I needed to practice more or was ready to perform the skill on a regular basis. If the attempt was less than successful, I would determine how many more times I would practice before I would test the skill again. Having confidence to perform the communication skill successfully helped me know I would be gaining more practice and success with each further attempt.

In order to improve your communication skills, it is imperative that you continue to practice the ideas shared in this book until they become permanent. You should not have to think about what an open-question is or what acceptable topics can be used as discussion starters. These "tricks" should be so embedded in your "communication skills toolbox" that they are second-nature when you are involved in a conversation.

OPPORTUNITY SECTION:

How have you grown from this communication experience?

_____

_____

_____

_____

_____

_____

List examples to show why more practice is needed or that you are ready
to perform this skill on a regular basis.

_____

_____

_____

_____

_____

_____

_____

What area(s) within the communication process do you need to practice?

_____

_____

_____

_____

_____

_____

List the skill(s) you are going to practice.

_____

_____

_____

_____

_____

_____

_____

_____

What strategy will you use to make these skill(s) permanent?

_____

_____

_____

_____

_____

_____

_____

_____

GOAL SETTING

"Goals give you more than a reason to get up in the morning; they are the incentive to keep you going all day."
—Harvey B. Mackey

"Decide what you're absolutely committed to achieving, take massive action, and notice what's working or not. Then, keep changing your approach until you've achieved what you want."
—Tony Robbins

"Write your goals down in detail and read that list every day. Then ask yourself, what can I do today to move closer to achieving one of my goals?"
—Jack Canfield

"Man is a goal-seeking animal. His life has meaning only if he is reaching out and striving for his goals."
—Aristotle

"You do everything better when you're thinking positively than when you're thinking negatively."
—Zig Ziglar

"The thing always happens that you really believe in; and the belief in a thing makes it happen."
—Frank Lloyd Wright

"Only those who will risk going too far can possibly find out how far one can go."
—T.S. Eliot

To summarize the quotes above, goal setting is a process that allows for achieving something to which you are committed. In other words, selecting a target you wish to change. Goal setting is an on-going process that needs to be constantly monitored as to what is working and what is not working. Using goal setting can help people reach individual targets.

Goal setting gives shape and the necessary direction to accomplish the achievements you wish to make. Successful goal setting allows you to improve something within your life that has a need to be changed. Change cannot happen without clearly defined goals. Goal setting is determining a current area for improvement; an uncovering process.

Within the goal-setting process, you must own the goal. Think about "personalizing and individualizing the goal". Building a personal connection will help you own the goal. The goal selected should be one that you want and need, not one that someone else has chosen for you or one that a friend might be doing. It is important that your focus be on the goal you want, and on the results being sought. The goal you set should be out of reach and require that you stretch to achieve.

Goal setting was a process that helped me decide what communication skill I wanted to improve and chart my progress toward successful completion. The setting of goals helped me focus my time and effort to reach the desired outcome. Through the use of goal setting, I was able to put my energy and time toward improving my selected communication skill. I also found that trying to improve too many communication skills at the same time was very difficult, and therefore, I would only concentrate on improving one or two communication skills at a time. Having a smaller number of communication skills I wanted to improve on at a time kept me from being distracted and allowed me to be more motivated and persistent in my follow up.

My first step in the goal-setting process was determining which particular communication skill I wanted to improve. Once my target had been set, I charted my progress on a weekly basis. Whether your progress is charted daily, weekly, or monthly, good and consistent follow-up can help you achieve the goal.

Another technique that helped me was setting a deadline. When I was working to improve my listening skills, I set a deadline of six months. Setting deadlines forced me to stop procrastinating and inspired me into action.

I also found that constantly reminding myself of the goal helped me to stay focused on what I was trying to accomplish. Sometimes I would repeat the goal over and over in my mind. Other times I would post a reminder of the goal. These reminders included posting sticky notes on the bathroom mirror, the front of my cell phone, and setting alarms on my phone.

Some goals I have made for my success never have come true. Does this result have anything to do with my confidence (I know I will succeed at…)?

On the other hand, some goals that I made were not successful. Was this a result of my lack of confidence (I cannot do this…)?

No matter which, we can very easily convince ourselves of our ability to accomplish something or be less than successful at accomplishing something.

If your goals are not met at your deadline for review time, do not give up. Instead, do something about it! Becoming disheartened and demoralized will not solve the issue, you must regroup and plan a different strategy with new ideas and techniques.

"When you break down large goals into small tasks and accomplish them one at a time, you will move forward much more easily. One great way to discover the individual steps in reaching your goals is to ask people who have already accomplished what you want to do. From personal experience, they

can guide you through the necessary steps and give you advice on how to avoid common pitfalls."

— Jack Canfield

OPPORTUNITY SECTION:

What is the first communication skill you want to improve? Why?

_____

_____

_____

_____

_____

_____

Use the progress chart to establish goals for yourself and to chart your success!

PROGRESS CHART

Goal Working On/ Deadline for Review	What Action(s) I Took	Results

PROGRESS CHART

Goal Working On/ Deadline for Review	What Action(s) I Took	Results

COMMUNICATION GOALS:

These are some suggested communication goals that can be used as you plan for improving your communication skills. Use these in your progress chart:

- Ask questions to ensure I understand statements and questions. (Ask the speaker a question about what he or she said to make sure you understood correctly.)
- Participate in turn-taking during conversation.
- Recognize my positive social interactions with others. (What did I do correctly during the conversation?)
- Recognize another person's social interaction with me. (Know when someone is talking to you)
- Demonstrate recognizing a person. (Call someone by name.)
- Initiate communicative interactions with others. (Be the one to start a conversation.)
- Observe someone else's use of a non-verbal cue and list what non-verbal cues you observed.
- Use a non-verbal cue when in conversation. (What non-verbal cue did I use to show the speaker I was listening?)
- Use a verbal and a non-verbal message to indicate to the speaker you are paying attention.
- Encourage speaker to continue talking.
- Ask topic-relevant questions to sustain conversation.
- Take turns during a conversation speaking on topic. (Statements and questions asked need to be topic-related.)
- Sustain a conversation by asking two or more WH questions. (During a conversation ask two who, what, why, when, or where questions of the speaker that are topic-related.)

- Maintain eye contact using the "three-second triangle" method.
- Do not interrupt the speaker. (Allow the speaker to finish speaking before talking or offering a solution.)
- Initiate communicative interactions with others by asking two questions.
- Reflect on an interaction whether successful or less than successful.
- Use a closed question to request information or assistance.
- Ask three topic-appropriate questions during a communication interaction.
- Describe the meaning of three negative non-verbal communication behaviors.
- Describe the meaning of three positive non-verbal communication signs.
- Identify and understand non-verbal social communication behaviors (i.e. Tone of voice, personal space, vocal volume, body orientation, facial expressions).
- Engage in conversational turn-taking with others across three or four conversational turns.
- Respect another person's personal space.
- Give a verbal or non-verbal response to other individuals initiating an interaction.
- Identify how best to respond to someone with a different point of view.
- Greet a person verbally or with a gesture.
- Initiate communication with another person.
- Take four back-and-forth turns in conversation with another individual.

OPPORTUNITY SECTION:

List any additional communication goals you may want to work on:

_____

_____

_____

_____

_____

REFLECTION—A GROWING EXPERIENCE

"We do not learn from experience...We learn from reflecting on experience"
—John Dewey

For me, reflection was the process where I would look back on my communication experience and analyze what had happened. Reflection was when I would actively and honestly think about the communication experience(s) that had occurred during my day. Reflecting back on these experiences allowed me to determine whether the communication attempt was successful or less than successful. Based on numerous communication encounters, my best results for improvement came when I would take the time to honestly reflect (look back). This reflection required me to analyze the communication experience and, to the best of my ability from an unbiased point of view (no blaming allowed), honestly write down the results. The more actively and honestly that I answered the questions also improved my communication growth and confidence.

On any day you will have many communication encounters. When you decide to reflect back, choose one particular experience. It is important that you honestly evaluate this communication experience to allow you to see growth (improvement) in your communication abilities. For me, after each reflection, I made it a priority to be sure to include notes/comments about the communication experience. (These included; a note of self-encouragement, something the other person said that I might want to discuss with them the next time I speak with them, etc.)

It is also important that after completing a reflection on a communication experience that you have a "take-away." A take-away is something you learned that could be used or not used again to help you be a better communicator. When the "take-away" was something I wanted to repeat again during a conversation, I would make a note card to remind myself. I've tried to always keep these "take-aways" someplace close at hand so I could refer to them. When approaching what I thought might be a stressful situation for me, I would remove my take-away card and glance it over to help relieve my stress and anxiety.

Example: I kept looking at my watch during a conversation with my best friend and our conversation ended abruptly. On my "take-away" card I wrote, "Less than successful—Try to not look at the watch so much."

Example: I smiled and nodded during a conversation with another friend and our conversation lasted longer than normal. On my "take-away" card I wrote, "Successful—Smiled and nodded during a conversation."

When reflecting, remember what Gandhi said, *"Be truthful, gentle, and fearless."*

OPPORTUNITY SECTION:

Use the questions below to evaluate your communication encounters.

For **successful** communication experiences:

What was something I did that made this communication experience successful?

_____

_____

_____

_____

_____

_____

_____

_____

What was something **I** said that made this experience successful?

_____

_____

_____

_____

_____

_____

_____

_____

_____

What was something the other person/people did that made this communication experience successful?

_____

_____

_____

_____

_____

_____

What did **I** learn (TAKE-AWAY) from this communication experience?

_____

_____

_____

_____

_____

_____

How have **I** grown from this successful communication experience?

_____

_____

_____

_____

_____

_____

Questions when reflecting on less-than-successful attempts;

What was something that I may have said/done that made this experience less than successful?

_____

_____

_____

_____

_____

_____

Was there something the other person/people did that made this communication experience less than successful? **(See "The Blame Game— How Not to Play It")**

_____

_____

_____

_____

_____

_____

What did I learn (TAKE-AWAY) from this communication experience?

_____

_____

_____

_____

_____

How have **I** grown from this communication experience?

_____

_____

_____

_____

_____

_____

CHAPTER 10:

COMMUNICATION CAN AND WILL BE STRESSFUL

When attempting to communicate with others, the objective is to have someone else understand the message that is trying to be conveyed. Unfortunately, there will be times when the communication attempts are less than successful. When this occurs, there is likely to be a feeling of failure. This "failure to communicate" feeling may cause the message sender both stress and anxiety.

For me, many of the times I chose not to communicate were when I was stressed out. This may have been my fear of not knowing what to say or the possibility that I would say the wrong thing. There were also times when someone was communicating with me, and I would "read" negative statements into their message. At these times, I would choose to immediately shut down communication.

Example: "That is a really nice pair of shoes you have on today." I was not sure whether to take that as a compliment or think the message sender was making fun of my shoes.

With my previous limited amount of confidence, low self-esteem, and not feeling comfortable communicating, these less than successful communication attempts would totally drain my confidence. No matter how much encouragement or support someone tried to provide me, it was not helpful and sometimes made me feel worse because I knew that someone else had noticed. It would often take me days or even weeks before I was ready to play the communication game again, and most of that "down time" was spent in isolation. This time was not only spent feeling sorry for myself but also trying to regain the courage and confidence to give communication another attempt.

There were many communication scenarios that I found to be stressful and I would try very hard to avoid them, sometimes to the point of feigning illness. These included speaking in front of a group of people, talking with my peers, or just having any type of social interaction that involved communicating with others. Although other people around me noticed these behaviors in my childhood, I did not become consciously aware of them until I started my high school years.

As I became more aware of my communication difficulties and my communicative behaviors became more influenced by them, a few of my high school teachers started noticing. Random comments were made either directly to me or my mom who worked as a secretary at the high school. Some of these comments and the subsequent actions taken by these teachers were helpful and others were hurtful. Without help from my homeroom teacher, Mr. X, I probably would not have made it through until graduation. He seemed to understand that I would always avoid going into the hall during class changes, especially after homeroom. Since homeroom was first thing in the morning and I had not yet prepared myself for maneuvering through the halls of Dover High without being noticed, this was a very difficult time for me. It was during the time when classes would change that caused me the most stress.

Mr. X would allow me to stay a few minutes after homeroom to help him set up the lab experiments for the day. He would write me a late pass to class after the halls were clear. If there were no lab experiments for that day, he would unlock the doors between the science labs, thus allowing me to get quickly to my next class before the halls became too crowded and anyone noticed me.

During first period, most of my "class time" was spent worrying how I would navigate the halls to my classes for the rest of the day. I became very good at helping teachers erase their chalkboards between classes and getting a "late pass" to my next class. Sprinting down the halls was also an activity I used to escape this stressful situation called school.

Comments made by other educators were hurtful and seemed to stifle any progress toward successful communication. A few teachers tried to advance my class participation by calling on me repeatedly, and when I could not respond either correctly or in a timely fashion, they called me unflattering names. I was advised, on numerous occasions, that I should withdraw from college prep courses and consider taking technical courses as I would probably be best working in food preparation or as an automobile mechanic and not having to interact with people.

I quickly learned that when placed in a stressful situation, I became less communicative. Stress became a barrier to my ability to effectively communicate. I chose to deal with this by not communicating at all. Instead, I became sullen and started isolating myself from everyone. This included family and my few friends. It would not be fair to blame my communication problems on my high school experiences, but I do think they were a contributing factor that exacerbated my communication difficulties.

OPPORTUNITY SECTION:

List communication situations that make you stressed.

_____

_____

_____

_____

_____

_____

TALK ON THE PHONE... NO WAY!

Have you ever made this statement "Do I really have to talk on the phone?" That was a statement that I had made many times previously. One of my many dreaded fears was of having to talk to anyone on the phone. I was not sure what to say to them no matter how familiar I was with them. When it came to speaking to people who were not family, or who I saw very seldom, my anxiety level quickly rose.

When the phone would ring and I would hear the statement "So good to hear from you, we have not talked in a long time", I would immediately try to find someplace to hide. This meant that some distant relative or acquaintance of my parents was calling, and I would have to talk to them.

When I did have to talk with them, I would take the house phone (the one with the cord attached to a wall outlet) and stretch the cord as far away from everyone (preferably the closet) and speak for the shortest amount of time possible.

In my teenage years, unless you were old enough to drive or had a friend willing to allow you and your date to ride with them, the telephone was the only way for young people to communicate. If you were just "friends" with someone, you would spend hours on the phone talking. For me, these conversations seemed "forced", often resulting in relationships that did not last more than a few weeks.

As I got older, people started using phones that they could carry around with them. Eventually, these devices became small enough that they fit on a person's hip or could be carried in a woman's pocketbook. Soon, these devices became so popular that everyone else had one on their hip, I decided why not me, and I got one. I found that often I really did not have a need for a phone except to be part of the "in-group". Once I got a phone and it did not ring much, I started wondering why I was not getting any phone calls.

When I did use the phone, the conversations were generally a couple of minutes long and very shallow. They would end with one of us suggesting we had something else to do.

What I later discovered was that, when I was on the phone with someone else, they felt that I was preoccupied or just not concerned enough to listen to what they were saying. When someone is fully paying attention to the speaker, this can be referred to as "being in the moment". My not paying attention and lack of participation or "not being in the moment" was causing people to not want to carry on a conversation with me. They were not interested in having a "one-sided" conversation or they would have gone and talked with some inanimate object, like a wall. There are some people for whom "not being in the moment" is considered rude and dismissive behavior.

Armed with this new knowledge, I started developing a plan for future conversations with others. My first step was to pre-plan my side of the conversation. I would have my side of the conversation scripted out. Many people told me that they felt I was reading to them, which I was. The important part was that I was no longer feeling anxious about talking on the phone. Explaining why I needed to script my part of the conversation and how it helped me, to others, made talking on the phone a more enjoyable experience. For the people who accepted this, I felt more confidence speaking with them, and those who did not seldom heard from me anymore.

They would have x'ed off their list anyway, now I was the one x-ing them off MY list. Spending more moments "in the moment" helped to improve my communication skills. Second, I started listening (previously I had just been hearing them).

Hearing is an involuntary physical ability involving the ears. Listening, on the other hand, is an active process and uses the senses of hearing, seeing or sense of touch. I found that listening was more difficult to do than hearing so I decided to make notes on what they were talking about. When it was my turn, I could "bullet point" the items I wanted to talk about. As I became more comfortable carrying on conversations, I no longer needed to take notes, instead, I just put into practice my listening skills. The third step was to start actively engaging them in further communication by asking open-ended questions about the topic(s) we were discussing. The concept of asking open-ended questions was discussed earlier in this book, but we'll also talk about it later as well.

Example: One day while talking to a friend, she was talking about her new shoes, and when she finished, I asked her if she liked this pair better than the pair she bought last week. She said that these were more comfortable and she could wear these to work. Looking at my notes, I asked her about the brown boots she bought last month and if it was her intention to wear those to work also. She replied, "Yes, when the weather gets colder."

She stated that, according to the weather forecast, it was supposed to snow on Wednesday, and she sure hoped it would, thus giving her the opportunity to wear her boots. Our conversation expanded into talking about the fact that we both liked snow, and how when we were younger, the snow was so deep that you could build snow forts. Because I had notes from previous conversations, I was able to remember things we had talked about before and this made our conversation continue for longer.

The second thing I did when calling someone was to have a list of topics to talk to them about or be prepared to ask them what they would like to talk about. I have learned that people like to talk about things that are important to them. When I would communicate with others, I would listen carefully to what seemed to be topics of interest to them. When the opportunity would arise, I would make a conscious effort to bring these topics back into our conversation.

What I found was that these practices prolonged the conversation and their use helped prevent many periods of silence. The people with whom I talked found the conversations more enjoyable and were willing to speak with me on a more regular basis. I found the same applied to me!

OPPORTUNITY SECTION:

Would someone doing these activities, during a conversation be "in the moment"?

- Vacuuming _____
- Multi-tasking _____
- "Glancing" at your electronic devices _____
- Making "eye" contact _____
- Responding to the speakers' question _____
- Reading a book, newspaper, magazine, etc. while someone is speaking with you _____
- Asking questions about topics or things they say _____
- Emptying the Dishwasher _____

USING HUMOR

When I am unsure about how to start or carry on a conversation, I may, as a last resort, choose to use a humorous statement. Laughing causes the release of endorphins which helps reduce anxiety and stress. Others are drawn to those who make them laugh and enjoy laughing themselves. For me, the use of humor was a great help when it came time to converse with others.

Choosing to use humor when communicating with others requires it being used in a very delicate manner. This means that whoever you are having the conversation with is not offended by your humor. When humor is used, it needs to be appropriate for the situation. In other words, when using humor, it needs to be at the G-rated level. For me, humor, when used appropriately, has many good benefits:

- Humor helped me relieve my anxiety and stress about being in a conversation.

- Using humor helped others reduce the stress they may be feeling due to the pressures of their job.
- Humor provided the ability to turn a funny story into a conversation extender.

Here are some successful experiences where I have used humor:

Example: In June of 2017, my niece, Melissa, announced that she was getting married and that their wedding date would be May Nineteenth, 2018 (My mom/her grandmother was born on that date). In December 2017, the Royal Family of England announced a Royal Wedding on May Nineteenth, 2018. Upon hearing the news, I texted my sister, Debbie, and told her "When you talk with Melissa, tell her not to worry because, after much thought, I have decided to decline my invitation to the Royal Wedding and instead will be at hers."

Example: As I was checking my luggage for a recent business trip to Florida, the baggage agent told me that my plane would be leaving out of gate B-12. I said, "that would be a good number for a vitamin." He immediately started laughing and replied, "I think it already is." We both started laughing and we talked for the next few minutes about a variety of subjects. Despite the holiday rush of travelers, by using humor, a conversation was started.

Example: I am a sports fanatic so people will often ask me if I played sports in high school or college. My response is that I was often encouraged by my teachers to try out for sports but I seldom made the team. One year, I tried out for the high school track team. My American History teacher was also the track coach and when I did not make the team, he suggested he could use me as the "javelin catcher". I was really excited about finally being part of a sports team and maybe earning a Varsity letter. When I asked him what he wanted me to do, he said, "go stand in the middle of the field and when the javelin thrower throws the javelin, I want you to attempt to catch it." After missing the first couple of throws, he cut me from the team. Apparently, I was not cut out to be a javelin catcher; I am not sure I know any successful ones, either.

Example: One night at dinner, I noticed a large family eating at a nearby table and attempting to get a photograph of their entire family. This was difficult because one person would have to leave the "family photo shoot" to get the group picture. I walked over and asked them if they wanted me to take a photograph of the entire family. They graciously accepted my offer, and I took a number of shots from different angles. One of the daughters asked if I wanted her to take a photograph of my girlfriend and I responded that I would have to decline her offer as I did not want my wife to find out I was out to dinner with another woman. Everyone looked at me in dismay and I quickly proceeded to tell them I was just kidding and invited my girlfriend to come over to the table. We all talked for about ten minutes before their dinner arrived.

Example: While seated in a restaurant waiting for our order to be taken, the waiter passed by our table and left a pile of coasters for our beverages. Joe grabbed the coasters and started dealing them out to those of us around the table. He first gave one to Kathy, then Aunt Mil, Shelley, myself, and then himself. I asked Joe if he had ever worked at a casino as he seemed well-trained at dealing cards. This resulted in a five-minute discussion about Atlantic City and the good times we had at the Steel Pier. We talked about the diving horse show, and the diving bell, all of which were attractions there. Aunt Mil shared a story about when she was visiting Atlantic City with her family to see a performance, her father made the entire family leave because the singer started fanning herself and he thought her actions were too obscene.

WHEN COMMUNICATION MAKES ME FRUSTRATED

When communicating with others, I most often become frustrated when I feel the person is not listening to what I am saying. I know they are hearing me, but they are not **_listening_** to what it is I am trying to tell them. No matter how I say it, how many times I say it, explain, and even re-explain, or give specific examples about the topic, they are hearing me and not _listening_ to what I am saying.

They hear my words but not my message. The person with whom I am communicating can always find an excuse for why what I am saying is not quite the way things are. Sometimes I feel the person is not taking me or my statements seriously or seeing my point of view. Too often, it seems the person with whom I am speaking is merely just patronizing me by hearing what I am saying and not listening to me. Often, when they speak with me, I feel they are talking down to me and they do not consider me their equal.

Example: When I am speaking, people will often interrupt what I am saying to make a counter-point. It is statements like; "You just never see the good things around you.", "I am sure that was not the intention of their statement.", "You always point out the negative things" that totally frustrate me when communicating with others.

Many people would rather talk than listen, therefore, in some conversations the listener is busy preparing a response and not listening to the speaker.

During a conversation, many people spend their energy thinking about what their response to the sender's message will be, they're distracted for various reasons, or they're simply rejecting the speaker's views rather than actively and effectively listening. One of the methods I have used when listening to someone talk is to think of myself as a juror whose job is to listen to the attorney make their case and not interrupt them with what I think is correct.

Often, during a conversation, the receiver of the sender's message is hearing and not listening. It is important to understand that listening is a more difficult process than hearing. During a conversation when you notice that you are more concerned about prepping your response than fully hearing what the speaker is saying, it is then that you have stopped listening instead of focusing on what the speaker is saying and you are focusing on your needs.

HEARING V. LISTENING

"Here's what I remind myself every morning: Nothing I say this day will teach me anything, so if I'm going to learn, I must do it by listening."
—Larry King

During our days and nights, we hear many different sounds, but we really only listen to certain ones. Hearing is much easier than listening because hearing is an involuntary physical ability involving the ears. No conscious effort is required, and hearing occurs automatically. As one of the five senses, hearing happens all the time and involves nothing more than our ears. Hearing is the involuntary receiving of sound vibrations or waves through our ears. Hearing is the "perceiving of sound." Hearing causes the speaker to feel people just "hear them". The common response when someone is just hearing the speaker is "I hear what you are saying."

Example: While I was writing this book, I could hear the fan blowing in the other room, the radio playing, the cat meowing because she needed to be fed, the humming of the refrigerator, and the neighbor starting his car. What I was doing was "hearing" those noises.

Listening, on the other hand, is an active process and uses the senses of hearing, seeing or sense of touch. The listener is consciously choosing what it is they want to hear. Listening is a skill that requires letting the sound go through your brain, understanding what has been heard, and processing its meaning. As a listener, you are understanding the information with both your mind and body. For listening to occur necessitates the listener's interest, involvement, the use of conscious effort, and a skill that must be learned and practiced. Listening requires being at a highly-involved level.

When listening, concentrate on the words that are spoken, understand information through your involvement in the conversation, and be alert to how the words are spoken. Think of listening as "paying attention to learn". Good listeners focus on the message the speaker is sending, and this can help build relationships. When someone is truly listening and says, "And how does that make you feel?", the speaker feels the other person "gets them". A good listener is someone who listens to what is being said, does not interrupt, finish their sentences or talk over them.

Sometimes people may need to just vent about an issue they are having and have chosen you as the person to express this experience with. Your duty is to listen. As a listener, it might be difficult not to interrupt by speaking or providing them with a solution. Paying attention to what this person is saying will be helpful to both of you. Your thoughts can wait… but listening to what the other person is saying cannot.

In summary, listening is an active process that requires conscious effort, involvement, and concentration. (SEE CHART BELOW.)

Example: During the same time-frame as above where I was hearing the fan, the radio, the cat, the refrigerator, and the neighbor's car, what I was also listening to and putting meaning to was the "Weather Monitor" alarm in the living room warning that severe thunderstorms were approaching and there was a flash flood warning posted until two am for the beach area.

Example: During one of my daily walks around my neighborhood, I heard a dog barking and then snarling. If I was only hearing, I would have made no conscious effort to "perceive the sounds" and continued walking. When I stopped and looked around for the reasons the dog was barking and snarling, I was making a conscious effort to "find meaning in what I heard," I was listening.

Examples of the differences between hearing and listening.

Hearing	Listening
Easy: Sound enters your ears—Accidental, Automatic	Hard: Practice, Attention, Being Alert
Passive: Involuntary, Effortless	Active: Conscious Effort, Focused Involvement
Physical Function: Involving the ears	Internal Behavior: Involves Mind and Body

OPPORTUNITY SECTION:

Are you hearing or listening during a conversation? Provide and explain examples.

_____

_____

_____

_____

_____

_____

List five things you will do to make yourself a better listener.

_____

_____

_____

_____

_____

Another time when I become frustrated during a conversation is when it is evident that the person with whom I am speaking is "looking to trade up." By "looking to trade up," I am discussing how the other person is clearly not interested in what I am saying or even talking to me, but instead is looking over my shoulder to see if there is someone else nearby who is more important or interesting that they would rather be talking with.

CHAPTER 11:

A GOOD COMMUNICATOR

A good communicator is someone who knows what they are talking about. You can recognize a good communicator because they are well-versed in their subject matter, and as soon as they open their mouth, they are speaking so that those around them immediately know what they mean. To be a good communicator, you need to intuitively make the receiver understand what you are talking about. They should know immediately that you possess the knowledge and experience to be speaking on this particular subject.

Have you ever heard anyone say "Do you see what I mean?" Good communicators are able to "paint" for the listener a description of their topic. They are able to accomplish this by the words they choose, their actions, and their passion for the topic. It is a combination of all of these that allow the receiver to clearly get their message. It's almost like you are inside their mind and seeing exactly what they are talking about.

Good communicators have learned the important skill of being better listeners. During a conversation, they focus on what is being said by the other person. They choose to listen more than they speak. Becoming a better listener may sound easy, but it is not!

OPPORTUNITY SECTION:

List five habits that would make you a better communicator.

_____

_____

_____

_____

_____

_____

_____

"HAS THE CAT GOT YOUR TONGUE?"

One of the many ways that communication can be ineffective is through the use of jargon. The use of jargon may cause your communication to be over-complicated or unfamiliar. Unless everyone already understands the jargon, certain people will be excluded from the communication. Those excluded may lose interest in the conversation because they may be trying to understand the jargon and miss the rest of the conversation.

Example: I can remember being asked as a child, "Has the cat got your tongue?" Since I did not know what it meant, I would fail to respond, and bursts of laughter would fill the room. This would then be followed by comments like; "You know Billy, he's just the quiet type.", "You have to watch out for those quiet types, you never know what they are thinking!", "If you would only say what is on his mind, you will feel better!" Not understanding the meaning of the jargon prevented me from responding. Had I known what that saying meant, I would have responded!

There are times when we say something to other people that may not be fully within their comprehension range. This may be because of their experiences in life, or a phrase they might not have heard before.

Example: At a recent speaking engagement, one of the other speakers made the comment, "Do not throw out the baby with the bathwater." As I looked around the room, one of the attendees had this puzzled look on his face. Since he and I had eaten previous meals together, he came up to me after the presentation and asked me if I could explain the concept. Prior to my explanation, he stated he questioned why anyone would throw away a baby, but after I explained the saying, he now understood the point the speaker was making.

The use of local or colloquial terms becomes especially difficult if you are speaking with or to others who are not familiar with the area or the language. Many misunderstandings have occurred because of cultural differences in addition to language barriers. Take, for example, the use of the word "bum."

One definition, according to the Merriam-Webster Dictionary, refers to "someone such as a hobo, one who sponges off others and avoids work."

However, in Great Britain, the word refers to one's backside. Neither definition is flattering, but it can certainly be said that one is much worse than the other!

Choosing what words to use is just as important as the tone and manner in which you use them. To quote Andy Rooney, the noted television journalist, "Keep your words soft and sweet just in case you have to eat them."

BECOMING A BETTER LISTENER

"If we were supposed to talk more than we listen, we would have two tongues and one ear."

—Mark Twain

"The word 'listen' contains the same letters as the word 'silent'."

—Alfred Brendel

Since we do not have two tongues and one ear, to become effective communicators requires us to become better listeners. To become better listeners, you should not talk too much, but take the time to listen to what it is others are trying to say. When people become involved in a conversation, it is not for the purpose of seeking advice or opinion, they usually just want or need to be heard.

Approach each conversation with the following thoughts in mind: What is the speaker trying to tell me? What "new" information will I gain from speaking with this person? Even if I might not agree with the speaker's point of view, I should still listen respectfully and perhaps gain a different perspective about the topic. Becoming a better listener can help prevent messages from being misunderstood.

These are the approaches I have used to improve my listening:

Prepare myself: Prior to any conversation, I found it important to prepare myself to listen. As the receiver, I needed to clear my mind and focus on the message from the sender. What I needed to do was think of this as my time to STOP and just LISTEN to the speaker. I found that, of all the communication skills that can be improved upon, the one I found most beneficial for me was listening. The ability to actively listen to the message being sent provided me the ability to more accurately receive and then interpret the message as the sender intended. I was also able to ask more topic-related questions which helped to sustain the conversation. What I had found prior to becoming a more active listener was that communication would break down and the speaker would become frustrated.

Too often during previous conversations, I found myself concentrating on my response to what the speaker was saying and not listening. In order to be a better listener, I needed to stop thinking about my response and consider any conversation I was involved in as a chance to learn something from or about the speaker.

Example: During a conversation with David, whom I usually only see at family events, he stated, "I just got back from a trip to China." I immediately thought that since I had never visited China but had always wanted to visit there, this was my opportunity to gain some information about China. I responded, "How long was the airplane ride and what sites did you visit?" When he responded, my next questions were "Which of those sites did you like best and what made them your favorites?" "Have you ever thought about living in China?" The conversation continued for about fifteen minutes. I viewed this conversation as a chance to gain information and prepared myself to listen rather than just hear him.

When someone is speaking, I focus my complete attention on the speaker and maintain an appropriate amount of eye contact. Both focusing attention on the speaker and maintaining eye contact when someone is speaking are crucial and important skills to becoming a better listener.

By focusing on the speaker and making eye contact, you are non-verbally communicating that you are tuned into what she/he is saying. Making the speaker the center point of your focus may help you remove any distractions that might be inferring with providing the speaker your attention. Because I know my mind can be easily distracted by other thoughts—did I feed Adidas, did I lock the front door, what is my schedule for the rest of the day—putting these thoughts out of my mind allowed me to better concentrate on the message that was being communicated.

Focusing on the speaker also reduces the chance of being distracted by activities that might be occurring in other parts of the room—people talking while the speaker is talking, someone shuffling through a notebook to find a clean sheet of paper, or someone entering the room after the speaker has started talking, etc. It also indicates you are listening and focusing on understanding the speaker.

I also found it helpful to position my body so that I am able to see the speaker's face. Previously, I would not have my body in a position that would make the speaker comfortable. Facing the speaker and looking directly at them (not so much that they feel stared down!) will help you focus on them and let them know you're actively participating in the exchange. When someone is speaking, it is important to keep an open mind and give them your full attention. There may be a conversation where you do not agree with the statement/belief/actions, etc. of the speaker. As a listener, do not make a final judgment until you have heard all the speaker has to say.

Be careful not to let one or two points you may disagree with distract you from the "whole" message. To help me become a better listener, I assumed that it was my responsibility to be attentive to the subject the speaker was addressing. It was not a case of just being attentive, but seeing the conversation as a chance for me to learn something. By approaching each conversation with a "learn something" attitude, I was able to keep an open mind about what was being discussed. What can sometimes happen during a conversation is that the receiver is not listening to the speaker's message but is instead preparing a response. Feel fortunate that they have chosen you as the person they want to have a conversation with. Be honored they have chosen you to be their "conversation buddy", and realize that you would want courtesy for your part of the conversation so you must extend that courtesy to them as the speaker.

Example: While attending an event, someone started talking about their religious beliefs and I was not in total agreement, I remained a good listener. As the speaker continued, I realized that a few of the beliefs in his religion were similar to my beliefs. Remaining fully present in the conversation allowed my tolerance of differing viewpoints to expand.

When someone is speaking, I found it important to not interrupt them and impose my solution to their problem. Sometimes people may just need to talk to someone about the problem without having any judgment made.

Discussing their problem might help them feel better because being able to share with someone else could help them see new ideas and viewpoints on the problem. They are not so much seeking for advice as they are trying to sort out the issue, thinking out loud, so to speak.

The point to remember is that they need to talk fully through the problem and share it without being interrupted. Interrupting and imposing my solution to someone else's problem was a listening trait that I was very poor at. When someone would start discussing a problem they were having, I would interrupt them and provide them with _my_ solution to _their_ problem. As you can see in the example below, it only took a few interruptions on my part to learn to let them finish before I offered any solution.

Example: During a conversation, my friends were talking about a problem they were having with the kitchen clock. They started to tell me about how their kitchen clock was not working. I interrupted them and told them that maybe they needed to purchase new batteries and I proceeded to tell them about these extra life batteries I had seen on TV. When I finished providing my solution to their problem, they both looked at me with a very weird look. They proceeded to tell me that the problem was that they had called two different electricians to come fix the problem and neither of them showed up. The reason they were discussing the problem with me was they were hoping I knew a dependable electrician. Because I did not allow them to finish describing the problem, the solution I proposed was not viable.

Becoming a better listener may require you to show curiosity in the subject being discussed. For me, this sometimes meant that I had to "fake it till I made it". Not every conversation I would have with another person would be stimulating, jaw-dropping, or contain material high on my list of subjects/topics to talk about. As the listener, instead of being bored, I tried to become "fully present in the conversation". I used the asking of questions to indicate my curiosity in the subject of the conversation. Often, a person becomes distracted when the topic is not, in their opinion, interesting.

Example: You are having a discussion with your sister who just bought a new pair of shoes. She has been talking and describing those shoes ever since leaving the store. What you are thinking, is "How many more times is she going to talk about her shoes! This is the tenth time she has told me about this same pair of new shoes! It would be more fun if we talked about a subject that I like!" Expressing any thoughts similar to that would end the conversation very quickly. As a 'good" listener and being "fully present in the conversation", you could ask her questions like "What outfit do you plan to wear them with?", "Are you planning to attend a special event to show off your new shoes?", or "What famous actress do you think would look good if she wore them?"

<u>When responding, stick to the same topic</u> (or "Being fully present in the conversation").

As the receiver of the speaker's message, it is important that, during a conversation, you listen attentively. Listening attentively provides you the ability to "reflect and respond" appropriately to the topic of conversation.

Example: During a recent conversation with daughter Kristen, she was talking about someone at work having a difficult time completing their assigned job responsibilities. When she paused, I asked her if she had considered the possibility of mentioning to her friend about enrolling in night classes at the local college. I told her that the newest college catalog had just arrived, and I thought that there was a course being offered that might be of assistance to her friend. Being "fully present in the conversation" allowed me to reflect on what we were discussing and to respond in a manner that showed that I was listening.

Example: Recently, I was asking a hotel clerk where the hotel golf driving range was, and she responded, "Last time I went golfing, I broke my finger." Based on her response, it was clear that she was not "fully present in the conversation". It appeared that she had stopped listening once the word golf was mentioned, and instead of listening to the rest of my conversation and the question I was asking her, she became focused on her golf experience.

The ideas listed above are important procedures necessary for making communication effective. When you as the listener focus on what the other person is saying, you are able to reflect and respond. Reflecting and responding allows for the continuation of the conservation. As the listener, you are provided the ability to ask pertinent questions of the speaker, gain insight or a new prospectus on a topic, and make the conversation become an information exchange session. This method also allows you the possibility to learn something new, and determine the purpose and scope of the conversation. Look at the example below at how quickly the word listen can become silent.

LISTEN

LSITEN

SENLT

SILENT

To become a good listener, one of the most important concepts is remaining silent.

OPPORTUNITY SECTION:

List three ways you will become a better listener.

_____

_____

_____

_____

_____

_____

_____

_____

IN MY CLASSROOM:

"Every man is my superior in that I may learn from him."
—Thomas Carlyle

Each of us can learn something from every person we speak with, we just need to be open enough to let the learning occur.

Although I used this example below in my classroom, I feel there are good communication concepts that are encapsulated within this example that you as a listener can use. When I was a classroom teacher, we would occasionally have a guest speaker visit. Part of each student's requirements during the guest speakers' visit was to complete the following five parts on a worksheet.

Every student would do EACH of the following:

- Look at the speaker.
- Ask at least one "relevant" question.
- Provide one comment.
- Provide at least one positive non-verbal cue to the speaker while s/he is talking.
- After the speaker leaves, discuss one "knowledge nugget" you gained from the speaker.
- Look at the speaker. When students looked at the speaker, the students had a "focus point" to help keep them from being distracted. This would also help them pay attention and listen to the speaker's message.

Example: When listening to someone, use the "Three-second eye method". The three-second eye method is that for three seconds you look at the speaker's left eye. After that, you look at the speaker's right eye. Then you look at the speaker's mouth. Then you return to the left eye, right eye, and mouth pattern. This allows you to maintain eye contact (or what appears to be near eye contact) with the speaker. This technique also provides the listener one less worry (where to look when someone is speaking to me) during a communication interaction.

One "relevant" question. As the speaker was talking, each student was required to develop a "relevant" question. By having the students develop a relevant question, it helped them to listen rather than wander off from the speaker's message. It also provided them the opportunity to "reflect and respond" on the topic of the speaker's presentation rather than think the speaker's topic had no relevance to them.

Example: During "Career Day" at school, people from many different professions would visit the classroom and speak about their careers. The most popular questions were "How much money do you make?", "Why did you choose to become a _____?", and "What other career choices did you think about prior to becoming a _____?"

Provide one comment. Each student was also required to provide one comment about one statement the speaker made. When the students were asking questions, they were interacting on a more personal level with the speaker.

Example: "I really liked the part where you talked about your dog "Meniscus!", "It must have been fun when you _____!", and "Can you talk more about _____??

Positive non-verbal cue. As discussed previously, non-verbal cues are "body language" that says far more than our words. During the speaker's presentation, each student was to provide the speaker with a positive non-verbal cue.

Example: A smile, OK sign, nod of the head, thumbs up, etc.

When someone chooses to follow these five actions, there can be a positive impact on improving your listening skills.

The chart below explains the effects for the listener and the speaker.

PROCEDURE	EFFECT ON SPEAKER	EFFECT ON STUDENT
Look at speaker	Has audience's focus	Follow speaker
Be prepared to ask one relevant question, and provide one comment.	Has audience's attention	Requires paying attention and receiving speaker's message
Positive non-verbal cue	Enjoying presentation	Focus on their non-verbal message to the speaker

OPPORTUNITY SECTION:

Use this chart when you have the opportunity to interact with someone.

Speaker's Name/Topic	
Did I look at the speaker?	
What was the relevant question I asked?	
What was the relevant comment I provided?	
What was non-verbal cue I provided?	
What did I learn?	
Did someone ask a relevant question or make a relevant comment that I would want to remember for next time? Write down what was said.	

A ONE-SUBJECT SPEAKER

During a conversation, some people tend to become one-subject dimensional and will repeatedly want to talk only about this one specific subject. Sure, everyone has a particular subject which they feel comfortable speaking about, but limiting yourself to being a one-subject specific can be a conversation stopper. As a one-subject speaker, people speaking with you do not want to repeatedly hear or have to limit their talking to just the one subject they feel interests you.

To be a better communicator, you need to assume the responsibility for expanding your conversational strength areas. Whether you are a speaker or listener, you should have known about more than one subject. Expanding your conversational areas will help allow you to more actively converse with more people and for longer periods of time.

One-subject speakers have shared their experiences with me about often feeling the person or people with whom they are speaking are looking around the room attempting to "trade up". Trading up is when people in the conversation look around the room to see who else is there. What is occurring is that they are ignoring the person who is speaking and checking the room to see if there is anyone else whom they feel might be a more interesting conversationalist.

Example: When I was young, I was totally fixated on sports, particularly baseball. I could and would quote anything about any player or team to anyone. Soon, the number of people who wanted to talk to me decreased or I would have people say to me, "Bill, I would love to talk with you, but I have no interest in baseball and that is all you want to talk about. Can we think of something else to discuss or I might have to go find someone else to talk with?"

OPPORTUNITY SECTION:

List the subjects that you think are your conversational strengths.

_____

_____

_____

_____

_____

_____

_____

List other subjects you would like to add as conversational strengths.

_____

_____

_____

_____

_____

_____

I found that once I started broadening my conversation subjects, my opportunities for speaking with more people increased. Listed below are some subjects and examples of some of the questions I used to broaden my conversation subjects.

Weather:

Talking about the weather is always a good conversation starter. For most people, some of their daily activity depends on the weather. People check the weather to determine what clothes to wear.

Examples: "That was some storm we had last night!", "Can you believe how hot it is today? "This is such nice weather. If the weather for the rest of the week is like this, I would really enjoy that.", "Did you see on the news last night that parts of Florida had several inches of snow?", "Have you ever lived in a place where the weather was different?"

Example: While attending my niece's wedding last month, we requested the assistance of someone from the hotel with our baggage. Immediately upon entering the elevator, he asked us how we were enjoying this rainy weather. Our conversation continued on until we reached our room. What could have been an uncomfortable few minutes between strangers turned into a relaxing exchange of ideas about the weather.

Sports:

Sports is usually a topic of high interest with men, and sometimes women, too. Talking about the game last night, the upcoming soccer game, or the game they or you have tickets for this weekend is a way to open the topic.

Examples: "Did you watch the Super Bowl?", "What is one sport that you do not understand?", "Who is your favorite team?", "What prompted you to like them?", "Have you ever been to a professional game?", "Are you going to attend any Spring Training games this season?"

Food:

It is difficult to find someone who would not be willing to talk to you about food. You might ask them about their favorite food(s).

Example: "What would you want your next meal to consist of?", "What is your favorite restaurant?", "Which toppings do you like on your pizza?", "Tell me three things you like about this type of food.", "What new food would you like to try?"

Pets:

Pet owners love to talk about their pets. Often, I will start a conversation with something my cat or dog did, and this usually causes a response from the other person about something *their* pet did. Asking someone about their pet is an excellent conversation starter. A majority of mornings consist of my girlfriend getting a call from her daughter about something their cat, Paisley, did. Usually, there are pictures also. There are many websites that contain videos of animals, particularly cats.

Example: This morning when I was making breakfast, my cat, Adidas, jumped up on the kitchen counter and started licking the pancake batter.

Example: "What is something funny that your pet has done recently that made you laugh?", "If you could get another pet, what would you get?", "Do you have any photographs of your pet?"

Technology:

As people become more dependent and the need grows for having more technological devices, asking them about technology is another good way to start a conversation.

Example: "What is your favorite APP on your Smartphone?", "Which games do you play on your phone when you are bored?", "Are phones banned in classrooms in your school?", "Does your school have a 'technology zone'?", "What is one thing that you would change about your phone?"

Children/Grandchildren:

Asking or talking to someone about the children or grandchildren in their life is another topic that can generate good conversation.

Example: When I am communicating with my daughter, Kristen, I can always ask her how Logen and Colbie are doing. I am able to find out about their swimming lessons, what they did at school/daycare that day, and how they are feeling. Usually we run out of time before I can ask all the questions I have.

Example: While visiting my doctor for my annual checkup, a lady walked in and when she opened up her wallet, a photo fell out. The desk receptionist picked up the photo and returned it to the lady and asked, "Who is that?" The lady answered, "That is my grandson. I have ten other grandchildren." She proceeded to show the office staff pictures of them all. When she finished, she showed them to the people who were in the waiting room. Some conversations lasted only a few minutes, while others lasted about fifteen minutes.

Example: "Do you have any grandchildren/children?", "What is one funny thing your children/grandchildren said this week?", "Do you have any photographs of your children/grandchildren?"

People's Occupation/Career goals:

Many people like to talk about the job they have or want to have.

Example: "What do you do for a living?", "When you get out of school, what type of career do you want to have?", "Is it fun being a _____?"

CHAPTER 12

SOCIAL SITUATION CONVERSATIONS

One of the biggest communication challenges many people face is the fear of entering into a social situation where they are not familiar or have limited familiarity with others in attendance. These social situations may include; family reunions, weddings, corporate parties, or a community event. In many cases, a person may face anxiety when they are invited. This anxiety grows greater when they realize they should or, even scarier, have to attend. Once they are at the event and have to become part of a conversation, they may then be at the level of experiencing a panic attack. Speaking from experience, these times were when some of my biggest fears occurred.

The technique I used to make these events less stressful was to "have a plan". This plan (thought out usually as soon as I knew about the event) has been very helpful and my stress and anxiety levels have been greatly reduced.

My plan currently consists of seven categories as my focus. I will provide a more specific explanation of each point following the list:

- Who are some specific people I know will be there?
- The location of the food table.
- The location of the refreshment area.
- Comfort level with hostess or host.
- Ask my friends if they are attending.
- Seeking out others who look uncomfortable.
- Having five or more questions prepared ahead of time.

Who are some specific people I know will be there?

Depending on the event, you are likely to know specific people who will be at the event. At a family gathering, you will probably know many of the people attending. Some you may see more often than others. I try to approach those with whom I feel most comfortable and will start a conversation with them. Since some members of a family are not seen on a regular basis, you might feel uncomfortable approaching them immediately as you might not be sure who they are. You could always ask the family members you know "Is that Uncle …?" or, "Is that really ___, she looks so different since I last saw her!" This allows me to speak immediately to someone I know and broaden my family circle as I get to know for sure whom each person is. Knowing immediately that I will have someone familiar to talk with helps reduce my stress and anxiety levels.

Example: A friend wanted me to join her at a special luncheon where her daughter would be recognized. I thought about who, besides her, would be attending and no one came to mind. On the day of the event, I spoke with her about meeting in the parking lot. When we entered, I recognized at least five people with whom I had previously worked and was glad I had attended.

Food table

I will usually, immediately upon entering, locate the food table. The food table is an easy place to strike up a conversation. Since most people like food, this area is usually full of people. I have also discovered that someone who is uncomfortable at social gatherings will be near this area. Finding who is also uncomfortable in these settings and starting a conversation with them can help make you both enjoy the event. Knowing that I will be familiar with someone else attending can help reduce my stress and anxiety levels about attending. (Little secret: it may be reducing their worries as well!)

Example: At family gatherings, there is always a food table set up inside, but outside is where everyone sits to talk. At one particular gathering, there was "the crab table". Knowing what was being served, I skipped the other food table for now and immediately went to the crab table. I started a conversation with my nephew and niece, and soon, other people joined our conversation. Later, I went inside and got some food. The anxiety of not knowing exactly what I was going to say, where I was going to go, or with whom I would sit was greatly reduced.

Topics for discussion at the food table can be as varied as the types of food being served, which of the foods would they recommend, do they have any specific dislikes for any of the food, and inquiring about their day.

Example: At our family gatherings, there is always a wide selection of food. Much of the food is hand prepared by Mom-Mom (my sister's mother-in-law,) who was born and raised in China. A conversation is always easy to start by asking someone which Chinese dish we are having tonight.

Refreshment table

The refreshment table is usually full of people already talking, thus joining into a conversation may be much easier here. As refreshment table items are usually not as elaborate as a meal, it is an opportunity for short interactions.

It can also mean that there are not as many items to juggle—drink, plate, utensils—and as such, people may be more inclined to engage in conversation. (If you find that your attempts at conversations are not successful, at least you won't be there long!)

Example: When I approach the refreshment table, I will look for someone who is drinking something unique looking. If I find someone, I will approach them and ask them what they are drinking and if it is any good. Their answer will determine if I order the same type of beverage or ask what other types of unique beverages there are available. Since I have already made contact with someone at the refreshment table, I now had at least one person to whom I could return and start a conversation. The conversation would be about the beverage we were both drinking or the different one I was drinking.

Hostess/Host

Finding the hostess/host allows me to thank them for the invitation and may lead to them introducing me to someone or maybe asking for my help. These are both excellent opportunities for meeting "new" people. Usually, during large "family gatherings", the hostess/host will be left alone while everyone else sits around and talks. Others may offer their assistance, but the hostess/host may politely decline the offer and suggest everyone continue talking.

If I am not involved in a conversation, I will go over to the hostess/host and start a conversation about how good everything smells and looks.

During this time, I will ask if it is time to prepare for getting everyone's drink order, or since I am already here, how can I help. This allows me to have a small conversation where I was the one who initiated, thus helping to reduce my stress and anxiety levels.

> *Examples:* "Thank you _____ for inviting me to this _____!"
>
> "Do you know anyone with whom I should talk?"
>
> "Can you introduce me to that person over there wearing the _____?"

Example: At a local event, I found the host and thanked him for inviting me and asked if there was anything with which he needed help. He stated that someone had brought a vegetable tray that needed to be taken outside. I took the vegetable tray outside and announced that there were some fresh vegetables if anyone wanted some. This allowed people to know I was there, and a few of them called me over to their table to talk.

Example: "Corralling the cats" is a term my sister, Debbie, and I use when it is time to get everyone from everywhere in the house to the dining area. Either she will say, "Bill, would you like to go corral the cats and tell them it is dinner time?" or I will ask if she needs me to go "corral the cats", meaning, is it close to dinner time?

Ask friends if they are attending. I will usually check to see if anyone I know will be attending the event. This allows me to plan to arrive around the same time they do so we can walk in together. Knowing that I will be familiar with someone else attending can help reduce my stress and anxiety levels about attending. Search out your friends who are also attending. Friends tend to know something about you and this allows for a more free-flowing conversation. This will allow you to speak to them, while at the same time maybe meeting other people. Knowing that I will be familiar with someone else attending can help reduce my stress and anxiety levels about attending

Example: You are attending an event at the library and notice that Kalpana is there and talking to someone you do not know. You should walk over slowly and tell Kalpana you are glad SHE/HE was able to attend and introduce yourself to the other person. *When doing this, it is important to wait until there is a pause in the conversation, or your friend recognizes you and invites you to join their conversation.

People who look uncomfortable. At almost every gathering, there are people who will be standing or sitting alone. This can also happen if you are part of a couple, and they know people there but you don't. Often, this happens at business events where one person of a couple works at the business but the other doesn't.

Business events can lead to shop talk, but if it's not your field or you don't know anybody, it can make for a very long event. The person sitting alone, like you, is probably uncomfortable in these settings and looking for someone with whom to talk. Although they may appear "unapproachable", they may desperately be wishing that someone would, at the very least, acknowledge their existence and help reduce their anxiety.

Example: Last month, I attended an event and noticed a man standing by himself and eating a cookie. He certainly looked uncomfortable and looking for a reason to leave the event. I approached him and asked him what kind of cookie he was eating and if he would recommend that I try one. We talked for about ten minutes and when the doors opened for Opening Ceremonies, we exchanged business cards and parted ways.

Have questions prepared ahead of time. Having a set of questions prepared ahead of the event was probably one of the biggest and best techniques I have found to help reduce my stress and anxiety levels about being asked to attend any event. Whenever I am asked to attend any event, one of the first preparations I make is to plan at least five questions that I know I can ask to anyone in the room. These are what I call my "safety questions".

Example: When I received an invitation to a large corporation's annual luncheon, my immediate reaction was I cannot attend! After some reflection, I decided to prepare some questions that I could use as conversation starters. I knew that there would be other people there, like myself, who were not associated with the company. The questions I chose to take with me to the luncheon were; "How are you involved with…?" If they were not involved with _____, I would then ask them "Where do you work?" "What part(s) of our job do you like best?" "Is this your first time attending this luncheon?" and "What is one small thing this company does that means a great deal to you?"

OPENING OR STARTING A CONVERSATION

When starting a conversation, it is important that you make a good first impression. It is usually in the first few minutes that someone decides whether or not they want to talk with you. The topic of discussion you choose should be generic and one that is not offensive. These are some techniques I have found that have helped me to make a good first impression:

Mind over matter—I have found that through practice, I have been able to put my fear away and successfully approach others. If you find yourself having difficulty approaching others, re-read the section on missed opportunities and do the exercise questions dealing with "what is the worst that can happen?" Some people call this the "fake it till you make it" approach. Remember that "Seeing is believing" and once people see you acting like a social person, they will think you are a social person. Once they begin treating you like a social person, then you will believe you are a social person.

Start with tiny steps—Tiny steps may lead to giant opportunities. There are many different methods to taking tiny steps. I have a friend who started out walking around the local park and would practice their communication skills by saying "Hello" to the trees. As this exercise became more comfortable for them, they would select a particular part of the tree and envision that as a person's eyes and both say "Hello" and make eye contact. For me, my first step was to hold the door for someone who was entering or leaving the same place I was. When they would hesitate, I would say, "Please, go ahead, and have a nice day." Usually, they would say "Thank You" and my response was "You Are Welcome."

OPPORTUNITY SECTION:

Suggest three or more different ways to open/start a conversation or interact with another individual.

_____

_____

_____

_____

_____

_____

CONVERSATION EXTENDING:

As you become proficient at opening or starting a conversation, your next step is being able to extend the conversation beyond a one or two sentence exchange. Being able to extend a conversation can help make you a more desirable person with whom to talk. People are generally more willing to have a conversation with someone they find interesting and with the same interests as theirs.

Examples of conversation extenders I have used:

"Yes, that is why I wore my favorite shirt!"

I had gone to the doctor's office for my yearly check-up and the nurse told me that I was going to have x-rays done. When the x-ray technician walked in, she said, "Today is picture day for you!" I replied, "GREAT... that is the reason I wore my favorite shirt!" This started a conversation about clothing that lasted the entire time I was having my x-rays done.

"I wore this shirt because I knew it would match the painting I would be purchasing."

At a local fundraising event, I saw a particular painting that caught my attention. Throughout the entire event, I kept walking past the painting looking at the prices people were writing down as their bid. With about five seconds left in the bidding, I ran over and outbid the last bidder, and being the highest bidder, "purchased" the painting. As I was leaving the event, a couple stopped me and commented about the painting matching my shirt. I replied, "I wore this shirt because I knew it would match the painting I would be purchasing."

"What is your dog's name?"

While walking around the housing development where I live, I encountered a man and his dog. I asked the man) his dog's name. He replied that his dog's name was "Maverick". This led to over fifteen minutes of conversation about the dog's name, how the dog got that name, and the movie associated with the dog's name. As I was leaving, the man said his name was "Goose", which caused a burst of laughter from both of us because, in the movie "Top Gun", Goose was Maverick's wing-man. It was not until a meeting a couple of months later that I learned Goose's real name was "Mark".

Below is a list of some words and phrases that can be used to extend a conversation:

- WHO?
- WHEN?
- WHAT?
- HOW?
- WHERE?
- WHY?

MORE ADVANCED EXPENDERS

- DO YOU HAVE
- ARE YOU

- HOW OFTEN
- DID YOU
- PLEASE DESCRIBE
- IF YOU
- DO YOU LIKE
- IF YOU COULD
- ARE THERE
- WOULD YOU
- PLEASE TELL ME
- WAS IT
- WAS THIS
- IS THIS
- HOW WOULD YOU

OPPORTUNITY SECTION:

EXTEND THE CONVERSATION.

"Last night I went out to dinner!"

Where _____

Was _____

What _____

Did _____

"I just bought a new video game!"

What _____

Have you _____

Do you _____

Where _____

Can you tell me _____

"I am thinking about getting a new job."

What _____

Where _____

I thought _____

How does _____

Have you _____

OPPORTUNITY SECTION:

Respond to these statements made by another person to keep the conversation going.

"I am so sorry that I bought this new cell phone!"

_____

_____

_____

_____

_____

_____

"I am not sure I like her anymore!"

_____

_____

_____

_____

_____

_____

"My dad is in the hospital. I hope he will be OK."

_____

_____

_____

_____

_____

_____

_____

"My day was so horrible all I want to do is go home and sleep!"

_____

_____

_____

_____

_____

_____

"The people at school keep taking my food!"

_____

_____

_____

_____

_____

_____

"I think I lost my wallet this morning!"

_____

_____

_____

_____

_____

_____

"My family is considering getting a new pet this weekend.

_____

_____

_____

_____

_____

_____

TABLE STAR!

Be the FIRST to introduce!

Have you ever sat at a table with people whom you do not know and everyone is sitting quietly? Sitting waiting in silence makes everyone uncomfortable. Seize upon this as your chance to be the "TABLE STAR". A "table star" is the person who gets the conversation started. The one who "breaks the ice" and helps others feel more comfortable. You can do this by introducing yourself, (Hi, my name is _____) and then asking everyone else their name.

A table star can also be the person who keeps the conversation going. They are the one who asks thought-provoking questions to keep the table occupants talking. They may also be the one who distributes information or collects materials as needed for the table.

Example: At the Future Farmers of America (FFA) National Convention several years ago, I was late getting to my assigned table and was seated with people from other states I did not know. I started by saying, "Hi, my name is William Lane, and I am a judge from the state of Delaware."

Example: I was scheduled to speak to a group of young leaders in the state of Delaware. When I entered the room, I saw I was the only person present. A few minutes later, two workshop participants walked in, sat down and started talking to each other. I walked over to them and introduced myself. They both introduced themselves, and we spent the next ten minutes speaking until some other participants arrived.

Other good "table star" statements are; "What does everyone do for a living?" or, "Are you a friend of the bride or groom?"

Try being the "table star" at your next gathering, rather than sit around waiting for someone else to finally make the move to introduce.

OPPORTUNITY SECTION:

What are some topics you might use to be the "TABLE STAR?"

_____

_____

_____

_____

_____

_____

NAME TAG DECORATION

When attending most events, people are asked to wear a name tag. I have found that, by not only putting my name but also including a symbol or something unique to my name tag, my name tag is a good conversation starter. When I am filling out my name tag, I put my name and will draw an "NY". People come up during a break or while we are waiting for the event to start and say, "Hi Dr. Lane, are you from New York?" I tell them I am not from New York but am a BIG Yankees fan. Their questions to me will be, "Did you watch the game last night?" "Who is your favorite player?" and immediately, a conversation has started.

By looking at people's name tags, I can find something out about a person and have something in common to start a conversation with them, or they with me. Throughout my various experiences using names tags at conferences, I have seen people placing many designs on their nametags. Some of the more unusual designs I have seen on people's name tags are: flowers, state shapes, names of their children, grandchildren or pets. When I first used this idea for attendees at my workshops, someone's nametag had their name and "1957". I thought that meant the year he was born, but during break, I was too intrigued not to walk over and start a conversation with him. He was not born in 1957, but instead, he owned a 1957 Chevy Malibu S/S. We spent the next fifteen minutes of the break talking about his car and looking at photos.

One person, who is a very good friend, always puts her nametag on upside down. It is an immediate attention getter; people will look and immediately comment "your tag is on upside down." The nametag wearer will smile and instantly comment, "Yes, it is a good way to start a conversation, don't you think?" It is a humorous icebreaker; everyone laughs, and any tension or uneasiness seems to melt away.

OPPORTUNITY SECTION:

What are some ways you can make your nametag memorable?

_____

_____

_____

_____

_____

_____

Use the space below to practice designing a nametag:

CHAPTER 13:

QUESTIONING SKILLS

The use of questioning skills is an important area within verbal communication. Being able to use effective communication skills is essential for interpersonal communication to occur. By asking questions, you gain answers, understanding, and maybe acceptance for the message sender.

During the communication process, questions will be asked and are answered to help clarify, extract more information, draw someone into a conversation, and as a method for sustaining a conversation. There are two types of questions that can be asked and answered, open-ended and closed.

Open-ended questions are questions used to solicit additional information. Think of open-ended questions as a way to collect stories rather than a collection of one or two-word answers. The benefit of using open-ended questions is that they allow you to find out more than may have been anticipated upon entering into the conversation. When open-ended questions are used, people often reveal surprising information. By using open-ended questions, you may discover more about a person's motivation, behavior, and concerns than was expected.

Open-ended questions start with "how" or other words that begin with the letter "w." These "w" words would include; "who," "what," "when," "which" and "where." Do not start open-ended questions with "was."

When asking open-ended questions, avoid "why" questions as a "why" causes people to make up a rational reason, even if they do not have one, to provide a response. It may also cause a person to feel defensive, as though they're expected to defend their response. Answers to open-ended questions require a lengthier response and have more depth. To test to see if your question is open-ended, try to provide a response using just a "yes", "no" or short answer. If a "yes," "no" or short response answers the question, then it is not an open-ended question.

It is important to use open-ended questions that are of a general nature. The question(s) asked should not be too personal. Questions such as, "How was your day?" "What is your favorite place to eat at around here?" are good conversation starters. Also, ask questions that encourage the other person to talk about themselves. "Does your dog always act this well behaved?", "What type of work do you do?

Example: "Where were you and your father going last night when I saw you?" Answer—"Dad and I were headed to the grocery store to pick up some carrots that mom needed to make our favorite dinner—beef stew."

The other type of question is a closed question. Closed questions stop the conversation and provide only the answer to your question without any further detail. The response you will receive to a closed question will be just what you asked. Asking closed questions will limit the listener's answer because they will provide no more information than is needed or required. A question that can be answered with a "yes," "no," or short response is a closed question.

Example: "What is the name of your dog?" Answer—"Fido"
"How was your day?" Answer—"It was O.K."

ASK OPEN-ENDED QUESTIONS:

For successful communication to occur, it is important that the questions that are asked continue rather than end the conversation. Questions that allow for the continuation of the conversation are labeled open-ended questions. Open-ended questions allow for the "two-way" flow of conversation. The use of open-ended questions has an inviting quality that encourages the speaker to provide a more authentic, in-depth, and lengthier response. When used in conversation, open-ended questions allow you to find out more about the person with whom you are talking.

Open-ended questions allow the other person the chance to talk about the topic rather than just responding with a simple "yes" or "no" or short response answer, thus inviting for a wide range of responses. Asking open-ended questions encourages others' thoughts and feelings to flow, allowing you to support this flow while gaining insight. When the speaker is asking open-ended questions, they are being provided the opportunity to talk in more detail about their interests and needs. Asking open-ended questions allows for further discussion or elaboration about the topic or for follow-up questions to be asked. In summary, open-ended questions provide a whole new avenue for further conversation.

Think of open-ended questions as the "essay questions" on exams you had to answer when you were in school, since they require a more detailed response. When asking open-ended questions, you are "bouncing the ball back" to the speaker. "Bouncing the ball back" to the speaker not only leads to clarification of the topic of conversation, but allows the listener to extract more specific information. When a person has the opportunity to think, they are more comfortable, and people who are more relaxed tend to be more forthcoming with their ideas, concerns, and feelings. Many open-ended questions can begin with "who," "what," "when," "which," "do you," and "how."

Here are some examples of open-ended questions:

- "Who do you talk with when you need advice?"
- "What are some of the things that bring you the most joy?"
- "If I were to travel to your state/country, what are some sites I should visit?"
- "What are some things that you do to relax?"
- "If you accomplished a large task, how would you reward yourself?"
- "How would you describe yourself?"
- "What would be your perfect weekend?"
- "What benefit do you bring to the group when you hang out with friends?"
- "If you could have any animal as a pet, what animal would it be?"
- "How would you handle losing your phone?

OPPORTUNITY SECTION:

List five open-ended questions that you might ask someone.

_____

_____

_____

_____

_____

_____

_____

_____

_____

_____

_____

WHO ASKS GOOD OPEN-ENDED QUESTIONS?

If you want to observe people who ask good open-ended questions, listen to news reporters. They are very good at asking open-ended questions because their job is to get the other person to talk about what they saw, think, feel, etc. The TV viewer is not interested in what the news reporter feels about what is happening, instead, they want the TV audience to hear from the people who were there. The interviewer leads the other person in the conversation.

Here are just a few open-ended questions that I have heard news reporters asking in the past few minutes while watching the news.

- Why do you think ...?
- How did that make you feel?
- What does it feel like to stand in 120 mph winds?
- How are you doing?
- Did you ever imagine ...?
- Why did you choose to ...?
- Did you ever think that ...?
- What can you tell me about?
- What has been the response since ...?
- What is your biggest worry?
- Would you recommend that ...?
- Do you think he should resign?
- How come it took so long for ...?
- Are you concerned about your future?

OPPORTUNITY SECTION:

Watch a news program and list five questions that were asked by a reporter.

_____

_____

_____

_____

_____

_____

_____

_____

_____

CLOSED QUESTIONS

A closed question tends to achieve the opposite effect of an open-ended question. What closed questions tend to do is limit the possibility for a sense of connection to develop between you and the person with whom you are speaking. When asked a closed question, people tend to refrain from elaborating on their response and instead answer with a one-word or short answer response. Closed questions are usually easy to answer because the responses are limited. It is very difficult to disagree with a person's answer to a yes or no question. You may not like the answer, but closed questions ask for a person's opinion and their answer may not be the one you were expecting. People may perceive closed questions as a statement, a request, a judgment, or a directive. Closed questions are similar to true-false questions in that many times the response can be "Yes or No".

Example: While I was waiting to get my haircut, this was the conversational exchange between a stylist and another customer.

Stylist—"Are you down here on vacation?"

Customer—"Yes"

Stylist—"Have the visited the boardwalk yet?"

Customer—"Not yet."

Stylist—"What are you and your family planning to do tonight?"

Customer—"Not sure."

Stylist—"Are you excited about going back to school and seeing your friends?"

Customer—"Sort of."

The next fifteen minutes of the young man's haircut were in total silence. As you can gather from this conversational exchange, when closed questions were used, there was little conversational interaction between the stylist and the customer. The customer was quickly annoyed with the stylist's questions, and the stylist was not asking open-ended questions to engage the customer.

There are times when closed questions are appropriate and necessary. Closed questions can be used to determine certain important pieces of information. This includes times when an immediate answer is required (for example; during times of an emergency).

Some examples are: "Are you injured?", "Where is the nearest evacuation route?", "Are you lost?", "Which way do I turn?", "Is there anyone here who knows first aid?", "What time does the train arrive?" You might use a closed question when you first meet a person, "What is your name?", or when you need to find out something quickly, "Is there a gasoline station in the area?", "Where is the nearest restaurant?", during times when an immediate answer is required.

The following are some examples of changing closed questions to open-ended questions. The first question, in each numbered series, is in the form of a closed question, while the second question is a more open-ended question.

"Were you excited about coming to this event?"
1A. "What excited you the most about coming to this event?"
"Who is your best friend?"

2A. "How did you and your best friend meet?"
"Are you mad at Diego?"

3A. "How did the disagreement between you and Diego start?"
"Where are you going on vacation?"

4A. "What sights do you hope to see while you are on vacation?"
"Do you think you can/will use any of the information you learned in this meeting?"

5A. "What changes will you make based on what you learned in this meeting?"

There will be times when someone may ask you a closed question. If you want to "keep the conversation going", here are some helpful examples of words (capitalized) that will extend your answer. Words such as because can extend a conversation past a closed question.

Example: What is your favorite color? My favorite color is yellow BECAUSE...
Do you like to. . .? Yes, and my favorite part is...

OPPORTUNITY SECTION:

Make the following closed questions open-ended questions.

The first two questions are done for you.

Q: How was your dinner?

A: What part of dinner did you like best?

Q: Whom did you sit with on the bus this morning?

A: Tell me three things about your bus ride.

YOU ARE ON YOUR OWN FROM HERE:

Do you play any sport?

Do you like to play cards?

Did you like the last workshop?

Can I help you prepare dinner?

Did you like the movie?

KEEP YOUR QUESTIONS POSITIVE

Whether asking open-ended questions or the occasional closed questions during your conversation, be cognizant that the questions you are asking are of a positive manner. Positive questions tend to keep the tune of the communication positive. People are more likely to respond to questions that are stated in a positive manner than those stated in a negative manner.

Example: "What three things did you like best about your vacation?"

When a negative question is asked during a conversation, "What three things did you like least about your vacation?", the direction is set for more negativism to follow. Once the conversation is headed in a negative direction, it may be difficult to return to a positive toned conversation. Negative statements tend to lead to negative thoughts! Instead, keep your questions in a positive light.

Example: "Would you like to go see a movie tonight?"

OPPORTUNITY SECTION:

Change the following negative questions into positive questions.

What is making you so angry today?

_____

Was that a horrible movie or what?

_____

What are the bad habits your boyfriend has?

_____

Did you ever imagine Sally would treat Tony like that?

_____

CHAPTER 14:

NON-VERBAL COMMUNICATION

*"Your words tell others what you think. Your actions tell them
what you believe."*

—T.D.

The outcome of one's communication can be greatly influenced by
non-verbal communication.

When someone is speaking, people may say "look at the words they
are saying." If you think about it, you cannot actually *see* the words they are
speaking but you can look for certain non-verbal cues. When someone is
listening, people may say "Actions speak louder than words." Again, this is a
reference to the non-verbal cues of the listener. Non-verbal communication
involves both the sending and receiving of messages, by two or more people
without the use of words. In other words, whether you are speaking or listening,
there is a need to be aware of your non-verbal cues. Knowing about non-verbal
cues is important because our non-verbal cues happen unconsciously.

Non-verbal communication cues include proximity to the speaker,
eye contact, facial expressions, tonality, gestures, and body positioning.

A person, whether they are the speaker or the listener, displays these non-verbal cues. It is almost as if their body language is saying "You should hear what I'm not saying."

The following percentages show what makes up what we say (verbal) and what we see and hear(non-verbal).

- Seven percent of the meaning of the communicated message is based on the words they used
- Thirty-eight percent is made up of the tone of voice that is used.
- Fifty-five percent is determined by the body language of the person.

That means that ninety-three percent of the meaning of one's communication message is based on how it is delivered, the sound of the words chosen, facial expressions, proximity, and body language. What this number tells us is that *how* something is said matters more than the words that are used. The impact that non-verbal communication can have on how one's message is perceived is extremely important.

Have you ever heard any of the following sayings, "Actions speak louder than words", "Judge someone by their actions, not by their words", or "What you do is what you say"? Non-verbal communication cues can be sent by both the speaker and the receiver. One's non-verbal communication provides clarity and depth to the communication. Be aware that non-verbal communication often happens unconsciously.

Non-verbal communication conveys powerful messages! Being aware of your body language can help you have more control over your non-verbal actions. When you are speaking or listening, it is important that you know what non-verbal messages you are sending. Many people do not realize the importance non-verbal communication has in the communication process.

Many people believe that non-verbal communication is comprised mostly of ones' facial expressions. One's face expresses their feelings, not only about others, but also about themselves. A person who is always frowning, has a mean look, or has a cheerful disposition is revealing what they feel about others and themselves. In poker, your face is your "tell". Someone is known to have a "poker face" when they show a blank expression to conceal their emotions.

Facial expressions are not the only part of your body where non-verbal communication occurs. Various other parts of the body can be and are used to express who we are and how we choose to relate with others. Non-verbal communication cues include our proximity to the speaker, eye contact (or lack of), facial expressions, touch, voice tonality or inflection, gestures, and body positioning.

PROXIMITY TO THE SPEAKER

Proximity to the speaker means how close we stand to the person with whom we are communicating.

Our familiarity with the person we are communicating with determines our proximity also known as "personal space bubble". When speaking or listening, it is important that physical distance and personal space is respected. People maintain an amount of space between themselves and others based on their relationship with that person. When we are speaking with a stranger, our distance should normally be about five or more feet of separation. For a casual friend or an acquaintance, the distance should be about four or five feet of separation.

With a friend or a co-worker, our distance of separation should be about two to four feet. If we are speaking with a friend with whom we are familiar, our distance of separation could be between two feet and zero space. Generally, people are more likely to maintain a closer distance to people they like. The knowledge, and maintaining and respecting of someone else's personal space are important concepts for good and sustained communication to occur.

A person's "personal space bubble", as talked about above and in the chart below, are the distances most people feel comfortable with when speaking to people in those categories.

Example: I tried to remember that when having a conversation with someone I would use the "hula hoop's distance" method to help me remember "personal space". This meant that I was inside an imaginary hula hoop and depending on how well I know the person, was where inside the hula hoop I would stand.

If I was not familiar at all with the person, I would imagine pushing the hula hoop toward the other person until my back was pressed against the hula hoop (keeping an entire hula hoop's space between the person and myself).

If the person was someone whom I knew just a little, I would imagine still pushing the hula hoop toward the person but keeping just a little distance between my back and the hula hoop (most of the hula hoop between myself and the other person).

For a friend or co-worker, I would imagine standing in the middle of the hula hoop (half of the hula hoop would be in front of me and half would be behind me).

For someone who I was good friends with, my positioning within the hula hoop would be that most of the hula hoop was behind me.

When the person was someone I knew really well (parents, other family members, girlfriend, etc.) I would stand to the front of the hula hoop.

Personal Space Bubble Chart:

Close familiarity with person	Six inches—One foot
Familiar with person	One—Two feet
Friend or co-worker	Two—Four feet
Casual friend or an acquaintance	Four—Five feet
Strangers	Five or more feet

OPPORTUNITY SECTION:

Answer the following questions concerning "personal bubble space."

What is the normal proximity range when communicating with a stranger?

What is the normal proximity range when communicating with a casual friend or acquaintance?

What is the normal proximity range when communicating with a friend or co-worker?

What is the normal proximity range when communicating with a person you are familiar with?

What is the normal proximity range when communicating with someone with you have close familiarity?

EYE CONTACT (OR LACK OF)

One of the ways non-verbal messages are transmitted is through our eyes. Much is revealed about our thoughts and feelings through eye contact. During social interaction, eye contact helps determine whether a person is paying attention and is actively engaged or whether their attention is directed elsewhere. People tend to find someone who makes eye contact with them to be more confident, interesting, honest, and likable. On the other hand, when someone does not make eye contact with us, we tend to think they are bored, deceptive, shy, or upset. During good communications, eye contact is required around sixty to seventy percent of the time.

A fine line exists between maintaining an appropriate amount of eye contact and staring. In order to maintain an appropriate amount of eye contact, I have learned to apply the "three-second rule". Anyone familiar with basketball knows about the "three-second rule". In basketball, it is a violation to stand in the opponent's restricted area for more than three consecutive seconds when your team has the ball. This is also called a "lane violation" (no relation!).

As a former basketball coach, using this term helped me associate something I was familiar with and thereby helping me improve my communication skills. I found that remembering and incorporating the "three-second rule" for eye contact technique into my listening routine was a good starting point. This rule also assisted me in initially making eye contact (a vital and necessary component for effective communication).

Those of you not familiar with basketball may want to use the "three second driving" rule. This rule of thumb, and a law in some states, requires a driver to maintain a safe trailing driving distance by keeping a three-second distance between themselves and the car in front of them.

The "three-second rule", as it pertains to the appropriate amount of eye contact, meant that I would look at each of the speaker's eyes for three seconds and then look at the speaker's nose for three seconds. There is no particular order in which I applied the "three-second rule" for eye contact. Sometimes I would start with the speaker's left eye, then make eye contact with the tip of their nose, and then to their right eye. It is important to be sure to find some method for making eye contact that is comfortable for you!

OPPORTUNITY SECTION:

Which of the following "three-second rule" examples will you use to improve your eye contact during a conversation? WHY?

_____

_____

_____

_____

_____

_____

_____

_____

Explain how this will assist you with making better eye contact.

_____

_____

_____

_____

_____

_____

_____

_____

_____

FACIAL EXPRESSIONS

Another important way we communicate to others is by the use of facial expressions. There are many times when our facial expressions can reflect our emotions. Facial expressions include smiling, blinking, and frowning. There are eighty facial muscles allowing for the creation of over seven thousand facial expressions!

OPPORTUNITY SECTION:

List seven facial expressions.

_____

_____

_____

TOUCH

Touch is used in a variety of ways to communicate our thoughts and feelings. Through the use of touch, we communicate to others what our thoughts and feelings are. A direct physical connection to other people is provided by the use of one's touch. Our use of touch communicates a message to the person with whom we are communicating. Touch can be used in a supportive or encouraging manner. Some examples of using touch to show we care and support others include fist-bumps, kisses, high fives, handshakes, pats on the back, hugs, and holding hands.

Example: When I see my best friend, Andrew, he and I will fist-bump as a way of greeting each other. For us, this is an indication that we care and support each other.

OPPORTUNITY SECTION:

List three ways you have or can use touch to show caring or support.

_____

_____

_____

_____

_____

_____

TONALITY OR INFLECTION

Verbal communication is about how you communicate your message. This includes what you say and how you say it. The use of voice tonality or inflection allows your voice to be used as a tool to communicate and influence others. Inflection is the emphasizing of the important words. Good communicators will use variation in their voice to get their point across more effectively and to better connect with their audience. Read the following examples and see how putting emphasis (inflection) on each different word changes the entire meaning of the sentence. Along with inflection, good communicators will use gestures to accent keywords.

Example: Read each sentence and notice how the meaning of the sentence is changed by the speaker's voice inflection. The statement the speaker is making is: "I think she is pretty."

"**I** think she is pretty." Makes the speaker sound like the only person who thinks she is pretty. Everyone else may not agree.

"I **THINK** she is pretty." Makes the speaker sound unsure if she is pretty.

"I think **SHE** is pretty." Makes the speaker sound like the other people around her are NOT pretty.

"I think she **IS** pretty." Makes the speaker sound like s/he is implying she was not pretty before now.

"I think she is **PRETTY**." Makes the speaker sound romantically interested.

Example: "I never said he broke our door."

"**I** never said he broke our door." Others may have made that statement, but not me.

"I **NEVER** said he broke our door." May have implied he broke it, but I never accused him of breaking the door.

"I never **SAID** he broke our door." May have written a note, posted, etc., but at no time did I say he broke the door.

"I never said **HE** broke our door." Others may have accused him, but not me.

"I never said he **BROKE** our door." May have done something else to the door, but did not break it.

"I never said he broke **OUR** door." May have broken other people's doors, but not our door.

"I never said he broke our **DOOR**." May have caused other damage to the house, but not to the door.

OPPORTUNITY SECTION:

Write a sentence and use your tone of voice to change the meaning.

_____

_____

_____

_____

_____

_____

_____

GESTURES

The use of gestures is another part of non-verbal communication. Gestures are the movements we make when we are interacting with others. A gesture can be made with our face, hands, and some other parts of our body. There are hundreds of different gestures that can be used depending on the situation, what message one is trying to communicate, and the person.

OPPORTUNITY SECTION:

List ten gestures that you use or have seen others use.

1. _____

2. _____

3. _____

4. _____

5. _____

6. _____

7. _____

8. _____

9. _____

10. _____

BODY POSITIONING

The position of our body can be used to indicate (non-verbally) our personality and our mood. One's body position generally impacts how we are perceived by others. There are many different ways our body can be positioned. Positioning our head, shoulders, arms, legs, etc. in a variety of ways can send different messages. If someone displays an upright body position when sitting, standing, or walking, others generally assume they are attentive and self-confident. When a person displays a slumping body position when sitting, standing, or walking, others perceive this as a sign of fatigue, weakness, boredom, or someone with low self-confidence. These are not always correct perceptions but remember that "actions speak louder than words". If you act in this manner, people will judge you by what they see you doing.

There are two forms of body positioning identified as, "open" and "closed". In the closed position, a person might have their arms crossed and folded, legs crossed or positioned at a slight angled open position away from the other person. A closed position may imply the person is not interested or is uncomfortable. Someone in an open position might be interacting in a more receptive position. They might be facing the person with whom they are communicating with their arms and legs relaxed and uncrossed. When an open position is used, the person may be implying that they are open to communication, interested, and have a readiness to learn.

Example: While speaking at an annual conference last year, one of the attendees sitting near the back of the room was slumping in his chair with his arms crossed during almost my entire presentation. Afterward, I had the opportunity to speak with him, and I asked him what he had learned from my presentation. Based on his body positioning during my presentation, I was expecting him to say he was bored and had learned nothing. Instead, he apologized to me saying that his flight was late and he had slept very little prior to attending my workshop.

Example for Improving Your Body Language—"Lava chair":

Do you remember playing "lava chair" when you were a young child? I can recall playing this game with my cousins, Linda and Kathy. The concept of the game was to pretend that the back of the chair was HOT lava, and whoever could keep from not leaning back and touching the "HOT lava" won. To improve your body language, when you are seated and in a conversation, (either speaking or listening), try to remember the "lava chair" game. Leaning forward and sitting up will encourage you to set your body at a position that is closer to the speaker or the receiver. The message you are sending is that you are focused on the subject of the conversation.

OPPORTUNITY SECTION:

Watch other people interacting and answer the questions below.

How close are they standing to each other?

_____

Based on their proximity, what is their likely relationship to each other?

_____

What facial expressions did you observe being used?

_____

What gestures did you observe being used?

_____

How is the other person responding to the gestures?

   Negative responses—_____

   Positive responses—_____

   NOTE—*Certain behaviors that people exhibit may not be non-verbal signals.*

   Example: Someone with their arms crossed may not be "sending" a non-verbal closed indicator cue, but instead, they might be cold.

POSITIVE AND NEGATIVE NON-VERBAL COMMUNICATION CUES:

Now that you understand the importance of non-verbal communication cues, review this chart about negative and positive non-verbal cues that are often used during a conversation.

Negative non-verbal signals	Positive non-verbal signals
Tapping feet while the other person is talking Arms crossed Legs crossed	Body in a relaxed position Open — facing speaker, arms NOT crossed, open hands
Looking away or staring at something/someone else (computer, TV, phone, band, etc.)	Eye contact with speaker
Not standing within a reasonable proximity of the speaker	See chart on p. for appropriate standing distances from speaker
No response to speaker	Asking open-ended questions. Where, What, When, Which, Do, and How
Not remaining still	Lean forward toward speaker (Lava chair)
Taking deep breaths while the other person is talking	Paying close attention to what message the speaker is sending

Note: There may be other circumstances involved that are causing the person to appear to be sending non-verbal signals. Cultural norms may influence the meaning of the non-verbal cues.

Example: The room temperature to them is cold and they are crossing their arms to keep warm. They are not purposely sending a negative non-verbal signal.

Example: In some countries, it is impolite to make eye contact when someone of authority is speaking to you. They are not purposely sending a negative non-verbal signal.

CHAPTER 15:

QUICK READS

What I have provided below are quick thought-provoking tidbits. These are intended as encouragement as you journey along the path toward improving your communication skills. When I read these in the morning, I call them "My Morning Motivators!" When I read them at night, I call them "My Next Day Motivators!" You do not need to read them all at once. Read one, and complete the opportunity section.

WE ALL STARTED SOMEWHERE

The fact is that we all started, or at least considered starting, the process of improving our communication skills somewhere, and possibly, for some, numerous times in the past. What is important to remember is that communication skills need to be improved a little at a time, "One step at a time", "One spoonful at a time".

Focus on the possibilities that can and will occur when you actually do make some improvement in your communication skills. Not only will you benefit from these changes but you will also improve your relationships with those around you, your family, friends, and society in general. Too often when people are considering a change, they focus not on the possibilities and the good from these changes, but instead, they spend their time and energy on the impossibilities.

Thoughts like; "I could never change these habits!", "Others said I would never be able to and they know me better than I know myself," or "The last time I tried to do something like this . . .I failed, so there is no way I am going to fail again." Anything that has happened in the past is not an indicator of what you are capable of now! Remember—Your past failures are just that, PAST failures, and in NO way indicators of your future success.

OPPORTUNITY SECTION:

Write down past failures that are holding you back.

STRIVE FOR WHAT YOU WANT

*"Success is not final; Failure is not fatal. It is the courage
to continue that counts."*
—Winston Churchill

*"One of the great discoveries a man makes, one of his great surprises, is to
find he can do what he was afraid he couldn't do."*
—Henry Ford

"Believe you have it, and you have it"
—Latin proverb

I was told by others that I would never have the opportunity to go to college because of my grades and inability to communicate with others, and that I should consider some other career pathway beside college-prep. I am glad that I chose NOT to listen to this advice and instead used this statement, and many others I heard repeatedly through my formative years, as motivating factors to "prove them wrong."

On the positive side, I told myself that I would someday write a book to help and maybe assist others suffering from the inability to communicate successfully with those around them. Guess what—You are reading that book! Usually, the things we fear the most…never happen!

OPPORTUNITY SECTION:

List the steps you are taking or planning on taking to improve your communication skills.

_____

_____

_____

_____

_____

_____

ACCEPT UNSUCCESSFUL ATTEMPTS AND MOVE ON!

Unsuccessful attempts are a fact of life! When you make attempts at being social or trying to "step outside your comfort zone," there are going to be both successful and less than successful experiences. It is important to remember that no one is perfect, and some of your attempts at communicating with others are going to fail. This does not mean that you are doing something wrong and therefore should stop trying. What is important to remember is not to get discouraged by the less than successful ones. Not everyone who attempts something is successful. Below is just a small sample of people who have faced less than successful attempts in their lives and have become successful.

Examples:
Walt Disney was fired, and his editor told him he "lacked imagination and had no good ideas."

Elvis Presley was told after a performance that he would be better off returning to Memphis and resume his former career, driving trucks.

Michael Jordan was cut from his high school basketball team. "I have missed more than 9,000 shots in my career. I've lost almost 300 games. 26 times I've been trusted to take the game winning shot and missed. I've failed over and over and over again in my life. And that is why I succeed." Michael Jordan

Winston Churchill failed the sixth grade and was defeated in every election for public office until he finally became the Prime Minister of Great Britain at 62.

Jack Canfield, the creator of *Chicken Soup for the Soul*, persevered through 144 rejections for a publisher. A series of books, *Chicken Soup for the Soul*, consists of inspirational true stories about the lives' of ordinary people.

You will also experience less than successful attempts at communicating with others. I have experienced many "false starts" and have used them to my benefit, to make my next attempt a more positive learning experience. One point that I cannot stress enough is that whether your attempt was a success or less than successful, take the time afterwards to reflect on the experience.

It's been said that we learn more from our failures than from our successes. It makes sense, doesn't it, that we would look into what went wrong so it could be fixed? If it worked, we'd just leave it at that, not questioning a success.

OPPORTUNITY SECTION:

List three specific improvements you will implement to make your communication more successful.

_____

_____

_____

_____

_____

_____

_____

_____

_____

DO NOT LET OTHERS RAIN ON YOUR PARADE

There are some people who hold the belief that making others look bad builds them up. People are quick to criticize something that they do not understand or that is different from their way of thinking. This author was told at least on two separate occasions, that I can recall, (I am sure there were many other times which I have subconsciously chosen to forget) that I was not good enough.

First, I was told that I was not smart enough to be in a particular classroom. As the attendance sheet was being read for whom was to be in each teacher's classroom, the comment was made that "Billy does not belong in that class, he is not smart enough." When I share this example with my students about the impact that words can have on an individual and how words can have a long-lasting impact, tears well up in my eyes, as they are right now as I write about the incident. These words were spoken over fifty plus years ago, and they still sting like the day they were said!

Second, I was told by a guidance counselor that I should not be enrolled in college-level courses but instead withdraw from them and consider taking vocational-level courses as my communication and people skills were lacking. The counselor was able to convince some of my teachers of this, and they tried to talk to me about my career choices. I was even assigned to "visitation week" at the vocational school.

I want to thank these people, those that I so vaguely recall making those comments or taking these actions, because I have chosen your words and actions as my inspiration to succeed in life despite the total lack of support or encouragement you provided for me.

OPPORTUNITY SECTION:

List comments others are or have made about you achieving success.

Negative comments –

_____

_____

_____

_____

_____

_____

_____

_____

_____

Positive comments –

_____

_____

_____

_____

_____

_____

_____

_____

_____

_____

WHAT IS HOLDING YOU BACK?

"Everything is difficult at first."

—Chinese proverb

"Once begun, a task is easy."

—Horace

"The beginning is the most important part of the work."

—Plato

In many instances, I found that what was holding me back from improving upon my communication skills was ME! Yes, I was my own worst enemy! In my life, I have experienced many "false starts". Instead of letting these experiences discourage me or even de-railing my attempts, I have used them as learning experiences.

One of the methods I have used to keep myself from becoming "my own worst enemy" is, after each learning experience, I analyze the experience. Whether the attempt was a success or less than successful, I would take the time afterward to analyze the experience. When you make attempts at being social or trying to do something outside your comfort zone, there are going to be both successful and less than successful experiences.

When you make these attempts, it is important to remember and celebrate your successful experiences. You may have heard the saying "success breeds success". Well, this is very true when trying something new. Often, not encouraging our successful attempts can lead to the demise of the planned attempt.

Equally important is to not get discouraged by any less than successful attempts. People tend to focus on the negatives, and when this happens, they feel that there will be more of these less than successful attempts at whatever the task. Life is full of successful and less than successful adventures.

Remember that not everyone is successful when they are trying something new. There is a possibility that this is something you will also experience. As you move forward with your journey to improve your communication skills, consider this; "What is the worst that could happen?"

Do not let the fear of rejection stop you from enjoying life.

Remember that you need to HELP YOURSELF! You need to be your biggest cheerleader.

OPPORTUNITY SECTION:

Write down past failures and explain why you feel they are holding you back.

_____

_____

_____

_____

_____

_____

_____

_____

List five ways you will encourage yourself.

_____

_____

_____

_____

_____

_____

_____

STOP SAYING NO

Another tendency that was holding me back was, since I know my communication and socialization skills were lacking, the word "NO" was my immediate response whenever asked to go somewhere or do something. My responses ranged from; "That does not sound like fun"; "But I will not know anyone there," and many others. After a while, I realized that by saying no too many times, the number of opportunities to participate in became smaller and smaller until there were none at all!

My current approach, one which I have found successful, is to follow this Dr. Seuss saying "There's always something fun to do when I tick-tock time away with you!" Just being with other people helped improve my communication and socialization skills.

OPPORTUNITY SECTION:

State three excuses you are using for not accepting an invitation to go somewhere or do something.

_____

_____

_____

_____

_____

_____

List three ways you can respond positively to an invitation.

_____

_____

_____

_____

_____

_____

_____

REWARD YOURSELF

One of the most effective methods I found for helping me improve my communication skills was by promising myself a reward when I successfully completed the task. I would reward myself for attending an event that I was not overly excited about (or dreaded) having to attend. When I started a conversation with someone I did not know, I would give myself a reward.

This reward had been predetermined and was something that was dependent on the magnitude of the achievement. You need to determine small versus large achievements, although at the start of my communication skills project, ALL my attempts were large. This provided me with confidence in myself and my ability to achieve success. As confidence in my ability grew, I started to categorize my goals based on small or large achievements.

For what I determined was a small communication achievement, the reward might be some snack or food that you do not eat on a regular basis. When using food as a motivator, I was careful to refrain from its use as my constant motivational tool fearing that too much success would lead to weight gain.

In fact, it did, because when I was growing up and went to Sears™ to buy pants, I had to shop in the chubby section. When I completed what I felt was a large communication skill achievement, making sure the reward fit the accomplishment helped encourage me to strive for the completion of even higher skills. One important point to remember about a reward system is that the reward choice must be something that YOU want and be desirable enough to encourage you to complete the task. Another important point when using a positive reward system is to remember that you must be honest with yourself, and only when the action is completed can you receive the chosen reward.

Once you skimp on fully completing the task but allow yourself to enjoy the reward anyway, you will have a difficult time returning to complete fulfillment of the task in order to receive your reward. You have, in essence, undermined the purpose of the reward system—full completion of the task in order to receive a reward.

Example: My parents used a positive reward system to encourage me to get passing grades in school. When I did get passing grades, my reward choice was, ready for this, an egg salad sandwich from the Green Valley Ice Cream Farm in New Jersey. While everyone else was having ice cream, I was having and enjoying my egg salad sandwich. As I got older, my choices for rewards are more varied, sometimes even ice cream!

Example: When I was first starting my plan to improve my communication skills, going to the grocery store was my "small reward". Knowing there was always something that I could reward myself with at the grocery store, I found it the perfect place to start. Many of my communication skills encounters occurred in the parking lot. Once during a rain storm, I noticed that someone was returning their shopping cart to the store. As I approached them, I asked, "Is your cart available?" He responded, "Yes" and I took the cart and headed inside the store.

Although my exchange was only a four-word exchange, which I had practiced repeatedly in the house and in the grocery store parking lot, I had made a successful communication exchange with someone so I headed to the vegetable aisle and bought myself a bag of carrots and some vegetable dip. Although this may not be your choice for a reward, it was mine. Remember, your choice for a reward must be specific to you, provide encouragement to go after your goal, and it must be a healthy and positive choice!

OPPORTUNITY SECTION:

List ten "small reward" items.

_____

_____

_____

_____

_____

_____

_____

_____

_____

_____

List ten "large reward" items.

_____

_____

_____

_____

_____

_____

_____

_____

_____

_____

REMEMBER POSITIVE ACCOMPLISHMENTS

It does not matter whether you make a big or small positive accomplishment, what is important is that you celebrate and remember your accomplishments. By celebrating and noting these positive accomplishments, when you have a less than successful situation, you can quickly refer back to the positive ones. People have a habit of focusing on the negatives in their lives and tend to forget all the good things they have that make them happy. Make it a habit to remember your accomplishments!

OPPORTUNITY SECTION:

List, in detail, five of your positive accomplishments.

_____

_____

_____

_____

_____

_____

_____

_____

_____

_____

_____

_____

_____

_____

BELIEVE AND PULL!

"You do everything better when you're thinking positively than when you're thinking negatively."

—Zig Ziglar

You must establish the mindset that whatever attempts you are making to improve your communication skills, you will be successful. Too often, people have the belief that they cannot do something, and as long as they believe this, it becomes true. Others believe they can accomplish something, and sure enough they accomplish the task. No matter which way you believe, the chances are, you will be correct.

If you do not pull yourself up…who else will? Remember, you are your own biggest supporter, encourager, and cheerleader. If you do not celebrate your own accomplishments, who will? Stop worrying about the purpose of a comment someone made; instead, focus on the reason it was said. Was it said in jest? Was it someone trying to use humor to relieve their own stress and anxiety? You need to stop taking everything personally.

What happens during a conversation, the comments made, or even the topics discussed may have nothing to do with you. You must remember that "It is not always about you!" This person may be having a bad day and did not want to talk with you and rather than say something, they choose to ignore you or say something inappropriate as a way of not talking to you. You have no idea what is going on in their life and you should not take it personally!

Another method I used that helped me was using an accountability partner. This is someone who is there to support you in the good times and the bad times. They lift you up and encourage you to try again, or they are there to celebrate your accomplishments with you.

There were many times in my life that I thought I could not do something.

Guess what—I was correct!

OPPORTUNITY SECTION:

List five sayings you will repeat to yourself to encourage your success.

_____

_____

_____

_____

_____

List three people whom you feel would be a good accountability partner. Be sure to explain to them what an accountability partner does and then complete the chart below.

For me, my accountability partner was someone who was there to support me in the good times and the bad times. During the less than successful times, they lifted me up and encouraged me to try again, and during my successful times, were there to celebrate my accomplishments with me.

Name of possible accountability partner	Why I think they would be a good accountability partner	Their response

TEN TO ONE

One of the strategies I learned about communicating effectively was the use of compliments towards others and also to myself. Everyone loves to be complimented, and for me, the use of compliments towards others proved to be a powerful conversation starter. What I used was the ten to one rule—ten compliments or words of encouragement for every one time I choose to share a negative comment.

Example: During an administrative retreat, one of the "ice-breaking" activities was to have a blank paper plate taped to our back. Everyone went around and wrote something they either liked or admired about the person. Although this activity occurred over fifteen years ago, I still have that paper plate, and I still glance at it to encourage myself when I am feeling down. Compliments do work!

OPPORTUNITY SECTION:

List ten compliments you could give to someone.

_____

_____

_____

_____

_____

_____

_____

_____

_____

_____

List ten compliments you will give to yourself.

_____

_____

_____

_____

_____

_____

_____

_____

_____

_____

STOP OVERANALYZING

When you choose to enter into a conversation, stop overanalyzing what to say or what others will think of what you contribute to the conversation. Remember that conversations are not about being judged for what you say but instead are an exchange of ideas and a chance to learn something from others. Approach each conversation as a chance to gain a different perspective.

When interacting with someone, remember that you *are* good enough or else they would not be having a conversation with you. How you respond to them should not be the qualifying factor in determining your self-worth. As long as your responses match your honest feelings about the topic of conversation, you should not allow this to inhibit your daily interaction.

Example: My friend constantly overanalyzes everything that happens or that she wants to accomplish. She makes statements such as, "Do you think that was the right thing to do?", "Should I have signed that paper with my full name rather than just my middle initial?", "Are you sure what I am wearing is appropriate for the meeting?", The word "overanalyze" begins with the letter "o", just as the word "obsess" does. Do you really want to spend time obsessing about the small things? You could spend so much time obsessing over the small things that you'd miss out on some pretty terrific things!

OPPORTUNITY SECTION:

What have you wanted to accomplish but have been held back because you keep overanalyzing the situation?

_____

_____

_____

_____

_____

_____

WHEN IN DOUBT ... SMILE

> _"Smile high! Smile low! Smile everywhere you go!"_
>
> —Dr. Seuss

When in a situation that makes you feel uncomfortable, I have found that a smile is a great way to help reduce the buildup of stress or tension. A smile will also help others around you feel more comfortable communicating with you.

Example: While attending my grandson's hockey practice, my three-year-old granddaughter commented to her mom about a man standing next to us. Her comment was, "Mommy, that man looks mad." When my daughter asked why she would say that, her response was, "Because he is not smiling."

CHAPTER 16:

QUOTES

Below are some thoughts to think about as you prepare for your journey to improve your communication skills. While some of these quotes have been posted in other sections of the book, others are new. The ones that I have chosen to repost are ones that I feel are worth reading more than once. A few of these I have made into note cards which I still carry around with me to remind me that my journey would not have happened without perseverance, determination, and a can-do attitude!

"Men fail much oftener from want of perseverance than from want of talent."
—William Cobbett

"Communication must be HOT. That's HONEST, OPEN, and TWO-WAY."
—Dan Oswald

"Communication is a skill that you can learn. It's like riding a bicycle or typing. If you're willing to work at it, you can rapidly improve the quality of every part of your life."
—Brian Tracy

"If you just communicate, you can get by. But if you communicate skillfully, you can work miracles."

—Jim Rohn

"The quality of your life is the quality of your communication."

—Tony Robbins

"Fall seven times, stand up eight."

—Japanese proverb

"Communication is depositing a part of yourself in another person."

—Anonymous

"The secret of change is to focus all of your energy, not on fighting the old, but on building the new."

—Socrates

"You miss 100% of the shots you don't take."

—Wayne Gretzky

CHAPTER 17

FINAL THOUGHTS

Here are some of the numerous comments I heard and experienced as I was trying to improve my communication skills. People would tell me "it cannot be done!" That it would "never happen!" "You cannot teach an old dog new tricks", "You are wasting your time!"

Let me tell you and them something, "Where there is a will, there is a way!", and I am an example of what can be accomplished. Life is too short to not be a contributing member to conversations with your family, friends, and society. **STOP BEING INVISIBLE!**

ABOUT THE AUTHOR

Dr. Lane has a long-held passion for helping ALL individuals to become contributing and successful members of society. This passion continues with his book, Stop Being Invisible, where he provides ideas, strategies, and techniques for individuals wanting to improve their communication skills. In this book, Dr. Lane shares personal examples of his struggles to become an effective communicator. In Stop Being Invisible, Dr. Lane provides the reader with first-hand accounts of fear, rejection, and missed opportunities because of his poorly developed communication skills.

William H. Lane (Ed. D. Widener University) was the Chair of the Master of Special Education Programs at Wilmington University (2003-2015). His primary teaching responsibilities were the graduate and undergraduate special education courses. Those courses included: Severe Disabilities, Teaching of Diverse Populations, Special Education Law, Applied Behavior Analysis, Methods and Curriculum, IEP Development, Supervision and Evaluation of Special Education Programs, and Assistive Technology. Along with his teaching responsibilities, Dr. Lane assisted in the preparing and supervising of prospective graduate and undergraduate special education teachers who were learning to teach such programs and also work effectively with students who had communication, behavior, and learning problems.

Dr. Lane has over thirty-five years of educational experience beginning his educational career as a teacher in both regular and special education classrooms. He served as a school administrator, campaign manager and then Chief of Staff for the Lieutenant Governor of Delaware, and as a university program chair. Dr. Lane was an adjunct professor at University of Maryland Eastern Shore in the School Leadership Doctoral Program and Delaware State University in the Education Program.

Currently an Educational Consultant, Dr. Lane works with the Delaware Teacher Center and school districts providing Professional Development presentations and workshops for educators. He was a presenter at the Eighth Annual World Autism Festival in Vancouver, British Columbia, Canada in October 2017, speaking on the topic "Closing the Socialization Gap". He traveled to Southern Arkansas University in April

2018 as a site visitor/reviewer with the Council for Accreditation of Educator Preparation Programs (CAEP).

He presented at the Milestones National Autism Conference in Cleveland, Ohio in June 2018. His presentation's title is: "Improving Communication Skills…Improving Socialization Skills". That same week, he presented "Improving Your Communication Skills" at the Yellow Ribbon Pre-Deployment Event in Tampa, Florida. In August 2018, Dr. Lane will be presenting this same topic in Jacksonville, Florida at another Yellow Ribbon Pre-Deployment event. Dr. Lane has been asked to present on the topic "Closing the Socialization Gap" at the Fifth World Autism Organisation International Congress in Houston, Texas in November 2018.

Dr. Lane's primary area of interest is assisting individuals with diagnosed or self-diagnosed Autism Spectrum Disorder (ASD) tendencies to improve their communication and social skills in order for them to become more fully engaged members with their family and society.

When Bill is not writing or presenting workshops, he spends his time between his homes in Delaware and Florida.

Author Contact Information:
Email Bill at: drbill22005@gmail.com
View Lane Educational Consultant website: www.DrLaneEdConsultant.com
www.StopBeingInvisible.com
Linkedin: https://www.linkedin.com/in/drwilliamlane/
Facebook: https://www.facebook.com/Dr-William-Lane-391158528078601/
Twitter: https://twitter.com/DrWilliamLane1
YouTube: http://bit.ly/2KGXjyL

TESTIMONIALS

"After reading an initial draft of Stop Being invisible by Dr. William Lane I wish to share my experience and take of the book over the last month while I read it and implemented its lessons into by daily life.

As a self-described introvert I have tried for many years to become a better communicator. In my attempts to accomplish this I have read many books on the topic and have come to realize that like any other skill, becoming a better communicator can be achieved by practice. Stop Being Invisible by Dr. William Lane was different from many of the other books that I have read in the past in that it provided a workable program though its "opportunities sections" where I could stop, work things out and then reflect on my past, present and future interactions and how I could improve them. I was able to take the lessons from each chapter and then immediately put them to work in my daily life. Whether it be initiating small talk with a waitress or store clerk, to practicing active listening during every interaction I found myself, over the course of this book, becoming a more effective and more comfortable in my interactions with others."

Sincerely,

Dr. Phillip J. Louie

"I recently had the pleasure of meeting Dr. William Lane who was a Speaker at the Milestones National Autism Conference on June 14-15, 2018 in Cleveland, Ohio. As Conference Director, I have worked with hundreds of speakers. I will tell you it was a joy and a privilege to have had the opportunity to work with Bill.

Bill is a warm, friendly presenter who is easy to work with and very dedicated to his craft. He makes the audience feel welcomed and at ease. Bill has a hands-on presentation style with well-designed activities that actively involve the audience and naturally creates a fun and engaging way for learning to occur.

Bill's session was overflowing! His topic of improving communication and socialization skills is of upmost importance to the autism community. Bill's real-life examples make his content very relatable to attendees. He did an excellent job of fielding questions from the audience and had visual supports to reinforce his material.

I would highly recommend Dr. Lane for educational trainings and workshops! I know Milestones is looking forward to future presentations from this dynamic, energetic speaker."

Sincerely,

Leslie Rotsky

Milestones Conference Director

"An extremely well written book on communication. Great personal insights on communication issues and very understandable examples of various communications situations. The author gives examples of what worked for him working with

students with communication issues as well as what worked for him dealing with his own communication issues. This book is great for educators who work with students with communication issues and for anyone who wants to improve their own communication skills. I very highly recommend this book."

William Messick, M.Ed, Special education teacher

Sussex Consortium

Made in the USA
Columbia, SC
12 November 2018